MEANT TO BE

A True Story of Might, Miracles and Triumph of the Human Spirit

To Davide,
Never give up!
Roslyn
Nov 7/21

ROSLYN FRANKEN

10-Q PUBLISHING

10-Q Publishing
info@10qpublishing.com
www.10qpublishing.com

Ordering Information:
Quantity sales. Special discounts are available on quantity purchases by corporations, associations, and others. For details, contact the publisher at the email address above.

Disclaimer:
Every reasonable effort has been made to ensure the accuracy of information contained in the *Meant to Be* book. Roslyn Franken cannot be held responsible for any inaccuracies, or the misrepresentation of those included in the *Meant to Be* book.

Printed in the United States of America

ISBN 978-0-9784274-1-2

*In celebration of my dear parents,
John & Sonja Franken - two unlikely
survivors of World War II who were
always shining examples of how to
appreciate life and keep going
despite suffering and hardships.*

*Dedicated to all my relatives who
survived the Second World War.*

*A tribute to all my relatives who died
in the Second World War who I sadly
never got to meet, but know they
are always with me.*

*In remembrance of the six million
Jews and non-Jews who died in
the Holocaust, and all the brave
Prisoners of War and civilians
who lost their lives while
imprisoned in Japan.*

Table of Contents

Introduction

What I'm about to share with you is the true and inspiring life journey of my parents, John and Sonja Franken - two unlikely survivors of World War II. It is an unforgettable story of war and survival, hope and miracles, and triumph of the human spirit.

While John is captured by the Japanese and must fight for his life as a POW, Sonja is taken by the Nazis to endure the horrors of Auschwitz and other concentration camps in Nazi Europe. Remarkably, John survives the Nagasaki atomic bomb and Sonja miraculously escapes death in the gas chambers on three separate occasions.

After suffering unimaginable cruelty with endless tests of courage and faith at the hands of their brutal captors, John and Sonja are brought together in the most extraordinary of circumstances to rebuild their lives as one based on love, trust and commitment.

In 1983, age fifty-six, Sonja is diagnosed with life-threatening cancer and expected to live for no more than two years. She dies twenty-one years later after a courageous battle that leaves her doctors completely bewildered. In 1989, John, age sixty-seven, must fight with all his might to survive a massive heart attack and emergency quintuple bypass surgery.

While growing up, I didn't fully understand how my parents' horrific experiences affected my upbringing and outlook on life. When I was younger, they were just my parents, like anyone else's. It was only when I faced cancer at the young age of twenty-nine, that I truly began to see my parents and their unique pasts through a new lens of reality.

When I share my parents' stories, people often ask me, "*How were your parents captured? How did your father survive the atomic bomb? How in the world did your mother survive the gas chambers on three separate occasions? What kept them going during all their years of captivity? Why didn't they just give up their will to live like so many others? How did they meet? How did your mother beat cancer so successfully for so long? What was it like growing up as a Second Generation child of survivors?*" Those who knew my parents personally ask me, "*How do your parents manage to be such positive, joyful people given all the horrors they endured?*" These are all questions that I will answer in detail throughout this book.

When I share their remarkable stories of survival and triumph, people repeatedly comment, "*Were they ever lucky. Talk about coincidences.*" Was it really just coincidence or sheer luck that both my parents' lives were spared in the most unusual and extraordinary ways that you're about to discover? My parents did not believe in coincidence or random luck. They believed that everything in life is '*bashert*' - a wonderful Yiddish word with different meanings, one of which is '*meant to be*'.

My parents' stories of survival are full of miraculous events, each one as uncanny as the next. They believed that each of the miracles bestowed upon them was *meant to be*. However, they did not rely on miracles alone. You will see how the miracles that saved them time and time again would have been meaningless and to no avail if they didn't play their part simultaneously. They saw their role as staying hopeful and mighty, daring and determined, and full of trust and faith that they would live to see another day and another and another. What I believe kept my parents going despite the losses, cruelty and misfortune they endured, was a powerful combination of their own courageous might, God's miracles and their triumph of spirit, all of which were simply *meant to be*. Hence, the title of this book – MEANT TO BE: A TRUE STORY OF MIGHT, MIRACLES AND TRIUMPH OF THE HUMAN SPIRIT.

Whether or not you believe in God or miracles, or agree that everything is *meant to be*, what this book asks of you is to simply open up your heart and challenge your mind to the possibilities. It invites you to consider what embracing this possibility could mean for you in how you overcome your own losses and adversities.

I've heard that children of Holocaust survivors, referred to as the "Second Generation", can be deeply affected by the horrific events their parents experienced in the camps, both positively and negatively. Therefore, as a Second Generation child, I'm here to share not just my parents' experiences, but also what I learned from them, and what I believe we can all learn from them and apply to our own lives.

I know, for example, that my parents' beliefs, values and attitudes have had a profound influence on how I live my life. In looking back, I can now see that it was only when I was diagnosed with cancer at the young age of twenty-nine that I first really understood how much I inherited their never give up attitude and belief that all in life is *meant to be*. Everything I learned from them was instrumental in beating my cancer and conquering many more life adversities that followed, including a painful divorce, financial distress, a bad car accident and the devastating loss of my mother to cancer, just to name a few.

The question one might ask is, *"If everything is 'meant to be', then are you saying that negative events are 'meant to be' as much as the positive ones? Isn't that just too easy and convenient?"* I will answer this very logical and valid question as well.

By sharing the events and personal reflections within the pages of this book, my goal is to demonstrate how the powers of the human spirit, choices we make and our sense of self-worth have no boundaries. We'll see that perhaps things happen that we cannot understand or explain, but are somehow *meant to be*.

My parents experienced and witnessed the worst of humanity first-hand. They were beaten, tortured, starved and forced to live and work in the most horrendous of living conditions. They were robbed of their loved ones, their innocence of youth, their freedom, their homes and all their worldly possessions, but what nobody could steal away from them was their will to live. Every day they watched as people died before their eyes in the most dreadful of circumstances. Despite all the horrors endured and witnessed, they never gave up their will to survive. Later in life, when faced with life-threatening health setbacks, they carried on with the same courage, beliefs and values. They never let their health issues beat them down. From all their past losses and suffering, they knew what it meant to just keep going, take life as it comes, and be grateful for every blessing received.

Whenever I go through difficult times, I remember my parents' experiences from which I draw great strength and courage. Reflecting on their experiences empowers me to continuously renew my faith that I, too, will overcome whatever is put on my path, and that perhaps my adversities were also *meant to be*. That is how I beat cancer, overcame my weight issues and thrived beyond other life adversities that could have gotten the better of me, had I allowed them to.

If in reading this book you gain just one new insight, inspiration or perspective that improves how you see yourself, others and the world around you, then you'll be able to help make this world a better place – a noble ideal we can all strive for, if we choose to.

My hope is that you will be inspired with a deeper sense of hope and faith which brings you to a higher place within yourself of greater strength, courage and determination. You'll then be better positioned to face your own life's ups and downs than you could ever have imagined. I truly believe that the more confident, resilient and healthier in mind, body and spirit that we are as individuals, the stronger we can be collectively for the greater good of all. In this way, maybe we can finally truly uphold the global vow of Never Again, and stop letting history repeat itself again and again.

The information presented about my parents is a comb-ination of selected stories they shared with me face to face, stories from my father's previous writings, as well as historical facts gathered through the internet for which information sources have been provided in the Endnotes section of the book.

John and Sonja were in two separate wars happening simultaneously in different parts of the world. Therefore, I will jump back and forth in narrating their respective journeys to help you understand the parallel experiences of their incredible might, wit and resilience in overcoming their insufferable circumstances. You will also be able to grasp the uncanny miracles that happened concurrently sparing them from death on numerous occasions.

I will share with you the following: a glimpse into my parents' childhoods until they were taken captive followed by key events that shaped their prison experiences and liberation;

insights into the unlikely events leading up to their meeting, marriage and my mother's courageous immigration from The Netherlands to Montreal, Canada; my mother's remarkable twenty-one year triumph over cancer, and my father's incredible survival of a massive heart attack and quintuple bypass surgery; the personal discoveries I made through my cancer journey inspired by my parents' experiences; and my own examples of unlikely events that I turn to when I need to remember that miracles do happen and everything is *meant to be*.

Part I

*From Childhood to
Captivity and Liberation*

Chapter 1

Good News Gone Bad for John

John was born on April 10, 1922, in Semarang, the capital of Central Java, Indonesia. Both his parents were Dutch-Indonesian. Indonesia was then a colony of The Netherlands, known now as the former Dutch East Indies. As such, it had a large Dutch population living there at the time.

When John was a year old, his parents moved the family to a small village in the South of Java called Purworedjo where they eventually opened a modest hotel called Hotel L. Franken. The

Hotel L. Franken

family all lived happily in the back of the hotel. John fondly remembers running through the grass in his bare feet, and playing hide and seek with his brothers under the coconut trees in the back yard.

John was born Jewish, but didn't grow up practicing all the traditions and customs of the religion. He learned much of his religious heritage through the many Jewish salesmen who travelled from The Netherlands to sell their goods and lodged at his parents' hotel. He treasures the memories of sitting on their laps as a young boy listening intently as they recited the stories of Chanukah, Purim, Passover and other Jewish holidays. He loved hearing about all the miracles of survival and the strength of his people in overcoming their oppression.

John didn't even realize he was Jewish until a terrible incident that happened in the first grade. He will never forget the teacher saying in front of the whole class to the girl sitting behind him, *"You see the boy sitting in front of you? He is a Jew, so if you want to hit him, you have my permission."* This was the first time John had experienced something so terrible. He couldn't understand why the girl sitting behind him would possibly want to hit him if he hadn't done anything wrong to her. He especially couldn't comprehend why she would want to hit him simply because he was a Jew. He didn't even know what this meant. John went home that day and asked his mother what it meant when the teacher said that he was a 'Jew'. She explained it to him as best she could. He quickly understood that it made him different from everyone else. He remembers how it alienated him from the other students and feeling deeply hurt by what the teacher told the girl sitting behind him. It was only after this first vile taste of anti-Semitism that he began to ask the Jewish salesmen to teach him more about his religion and the history of his people.

John had four brothers and was the second youngest of the five boys. His older brother, Paul, was the first to get married. The only problem was that there were no Rabbis in the Dutch East Indies to perform the religious wedding ceremony. Paul wrote a letter to a Rabbi in The Netherlands asking for advice. He was promptly advised that any pious Jew could perform the ceremony. That's when they heard of a Mr. Van der Velde who qualified and would gladly perform the ceremony. Mr. and Mrs. Van der Velde became good friends of John's family. Little did John know at the time how Mrs. Van der Velde would later in years play a very important role in his own adult life and future.

John's father, Leopold, died in 1940 of blood poisoning. On his deathbed, he called his two youngest boys, John and Albert, to his bedside and said to them, *"Be sure to learn a good trade my sons. That way you will never go hungry."* John would never forget those words.

In 1940, John proudly celebrated his eighteenth birthday. He was a bit of a chubby child growing up, but by the time he was eighteen, he had slimmed down and grown into a good looking young man. He had a head of thick, dark hair as beautiful as his warm smile and kind brown eyes.

Having just graduated from technical school where he learned how to weld and work on a lathe, he now longed for independence, eager to learn a specialized trade just like his father advised him so he could make a good life for himself, get married and raise a family. This was his dream. That's when John got the good news.

He received his letter of conscription from the Dutch Navy Air Force to report for duty in Surabaya. There he would finally learn a trade as an aircraft carrier mechanic. John was so excited. He was not very tall at only 5 feet and 5 inches, but at this moment he may as well have been 10 feet tall. That's what he felt like on the inside. He saw this letter as his ticket to freedom. It meant that he was finally going to move away from home, learn a trade and start a new life as an independent adult. This would bring him one step closer to living his dream of getting married and raising a family.

John ran outside to tell his mother who was busy hanging laundry on the clothesline. Rosetta was a short and gentle woman who loved all her boys the same. Three of the other four boys had already left home, and with her husband's recent passing, John now leaving, and her youngest joining the army, I can only imagine how difficult this must have been for her to learn of John's conscription. She was left behind unsure of when she would see young John or any of her other beloved boys again.

John's parents: Rosetta and Leopold Franken

John packed some basic belongings and travelled to Surabaya full of enthusiasm and ready to report for duty. The training began immediately. There was so much to learn, but John loved learning and absorbed it all like a sponge showing a natural aptitude for the trade.

After eight months of training, on December 8, 1941, John's dreams of independence, freedom, getting married and starting a family came to a complete halt. That was the day the war broke out in the Far East. It was the day that changed the course of John's life forever.

With the declaration of war, John learned for the first of many times thereafter, how life as you know it can change on a dime - just like that. He would tell you from his experiences how *"things can just change overnight"*. This was the first time that John's life would be at stake. He had no idea what was yet to come.

Escaping the Enemy

Frightened for their lives, John and his division were ordered to prepare for emergency evacuation. In desperate need to use the washroom, John rushed into one of the outhouses close by the bomb shelter. As he sat on the toilet, the bomb siren went off unexpectedly to signal the enemy planes fast approaching. In a panic, he hurried to get to the bomb shelter, running for his life while frantically struggling to pull up his pants. He dove toward the bomb shelter and made it to safety just in time. Safe in the bomb shelter, John remembers catching his breath surrounded by his buddies who all sighed with relief that he made it to the bomb shelter alive.

When the bombing ceased and quiet returned, the boys exited the bomb shelter. John looked at the row of outhouses, and to his disbelief saw that the toilet he was sitting on just moments prior was the only one demolished by the bomb. He remembers his knees growing weak as the reality hit of how narrowly he escaped death. He looked up to the sky, put his hands together and thanked God for sparing his life.

In telling me this story, he recalled how this was the first of many times that his life was saved by what he calls a miracle. He felt that the split second timing was too uncanny for it to be a mere coincidence. Maybe it was just good luck, but my father is convinced that it was *meant to be*. Looking back at that moment, he feels in his heart that he was simply meant to live and not die. To what purpose, John did not know, but he believed only time would tell.

John and his comrades were loaded onto a bus for evacuation to Chilachap - a port city in the southern part of Java. The native bus driver, unable to cope with his own fear, abandoned the bus without notice, leaving all the boys stranded in the middle of nowhere. John and his mates were scared and confused, not knowing how to react and what to do next.

One of his buddies stepped up and volunteered to take over the steering wheel. There was only one problem - nobody knew how to get from where they were to where they were going. They didn't have a map and all the road signs had been removed. To conquer these obstacles, each time they went through a new section of the countryside, a different boy would guide the driver for the particular areas which he knew best.

The driver stopped in each boy's village along the way so they could say good-bye to their families. This gave John an opportunity to say a proper farewell to his mother, not knowing if this would be the last time he would see her. He hugged and kissed her good-bye, assuring her that everything will be okay, even though he knew deep in his heart that he may never see her again. He still remembers waving his final good-bye from the bus till they were finally out of each other's view. As fate would have it, this was in fact the last time John would ever see his mother alive. He told me that the driver abandoning the bus was *meant to be*. If this didn't happen, my father may never have had the opportunity to say his final good-bye to his mother.

With this attitude, he was grateful to the driver who abandoned the bus. Believing that it was *meant to be* allowed him to see the positive outcome of what at first seemed like a terrible turn of events. This is a great example of how in life sometimes there are difficult setbacks put before us that when looking back we can see the positive impacts as we move forward. It is also a miracle that they managed to find their way to the port without a map, directions, or even road signs.

Upon arrival at Chilachap, John and his mates immediately boarded a ship to escape the Japanese enemy. There were two ships to choose from; the *Kotabarou* and the *Tjeiroasa*. How were they supposed to choose which ship to board? John and five of his closest buddies got together to make a decision. They chose the *Tjeiroasa* because it was the ship designated for their supervisors, officers, corporals and sergeants. Their thinking was that if they went with the *"big shots,"* as he called them, maybe they'd get better food.

John's ship, headed for freedom in Australia where he was to finish his training, sadly never made it there. This, too, must have been *meant to be*. Had my dad chosen the other ship, what direction would his life have taken? Would I even be here writing to you right now? One will never know. All we know is that this was the fate that my father was dealt.

Captured at Sea

At 2:00pm that afternoon, standing on the deck of the ship, John looked to the sky and saw a Japanese fighter plane approaching. It flew overhead with no incident. He breathed a sigh of relief thinking that his life was spared and their ship was safe.

Later that day, John and his mates suddenly saw Japanese cruisers in the distance fast approaching with torpedoes pointing straight at their ship. John and three of his buddies, hopeful and determined, hurried to the other side of the ship where they planned to jump off to safety. Unfortunately, when they got there and looked down at the water, they saw a school of sharks swimming in circles.

John looked down at the sharks and then back at the Japanese cruisers who were now circling their ship like sharks. With nothing but their old style guns for protection and a crushing sense of defeat, John and the three other boys chose not to jump.

The Japanese captain came aboard the ship and shouted, *"You are all now Prisoners of War. You all have to follow orders from me now and anyone not following orders will be shot".*

With that declaration, John and his mates instantly became POWs (Prisoners of War). John had no idea of what this fate would mean for the next three and a half years of his life.

Chapter 2

Loss of Innocence for Sonja

My dear mother was born as Schoontje Pagrach on February 6, 1926, in Rijssen, a quaint town in the province of Overijssel in The Netherlands. It was only after the war that she became known as Sonja. As I have always known my mother as Sonja, I will refer to her as Sonja.

Her father, Abraham, was a kosher butcher and her mother, Mittje, stayed home to raise the children and manage the household.

Sonja's parents: Abraham and Mittje Pagrach

Sonja was raised in a traditional Jewish home where the Sabbath, holidays and laws of the Torah were observed with great joy, devotion and respect.

My mother loved to sing all the prayers, especially those of the Passover Seder. She had a natural, beautiful singing voice which played an important role in her youth and throughout her adult life. When she had trouble falling asleep as a young child, she remembers singing herself to sleep. Singing, she told me, was what always made her feel safe and alive. It was what fed her soul no matter what else was happening around her.

Sonja was closest to her older sister, Ro, who was exactly ten years older to the day. She always looked up to Ro and loved her dearly.

Sonja's sister Ro

She had a fraternal twin sister, Ali, and one more sister, Johanna. Sadly, I do not have a photo of Johanna.

Left: Ali Right: Sonja

She also had two brothers, Manuel and Samuel.

Sonja's brother Manuel

Sonja's brother Samuel
Notice the Star of David sewn onto his left suit pocket.
All Jews had to sew a Star of David into their clothing as identification.

Just before the war, Ro planned to marry a man named Hans who she loved deeply. Sonja looked forward to singing at their wedding. Sadly, when Germany finally occupied my mother's town, Hans was taken away by the Nazis never to be seen again. This broke Ro's heart. She learned after the war that he died in Auschwitz.

Sonja had a crush on Hans. She used to tell Ro, *"If you don't marry Hans, I will."* Unfortunately, Sonja would never get to sing at the wedding. She was deeply saddened to later learn of his tragic fate.

My mother was the kind of person who never stood for nonsense. I remember her telling me the story of when she had lice as a young girl in elementary school. It was so bad that her mother shaved Sonja's hair off and made her wear a hat to cover her bald head. Of course, this gave the schoolyard bullies a great incentive to say mean things, laugh at her and try to take off her hat. Finally, when enough was enough, Sonja went back to the classroom and asked the teacher if she could speak to the class. With the teacher's permission, she stood in front of the class, all of eleven years old at the time, and with great courage and indignation simply pulled the hat off in front of everyone. Holding the hat high above her head, she said, *"Here. Now you know why I'm wearing a hat. Are you happy now? Maybe you'll be next to have lice and you too will be bald like I am now. Then we'll see if you're still laughing."* That took care of the bullying. Everyone respected her after that and stopped trying to pull off her hat. The mystery was solved.

I think about that event and how much of a statement it makes of the fearlessness that my small but mighty mother showed at such a young age. She had no way of knowing that this would be the first of many times she would be bald during the course of her life. I truly believe that the same courage is what helped her survive the war, beat cancer and overcome many other life adversities.

Sonja's Capture

One day, age fifteen, Sonja looked out her living room window and saw endless rows of Nazi soldiers marching through the cobblestone streets of her little town. They were all in uniform, marching in unison with their harsh faces, straight backs and high black boots. She will never forget that frightening sight and the threatening sound of their boots hitting the pavement with every step. Her quaint little town was being occupied by the Nazis.

All of a sudden, a herd of Nazis burst through the door. They forced my mother and her family out of their home and took them to the Vught concentration camp, a transit camp in the South of The Netherlands. The camp measured 500 by 200 meters and consisted of thirty-six living and twenty-three working barracks. A double barbed-wire fence with a ditch between them surrounded the camp. Watchtowers were placed every 50 meters around the perimeter. Situated outside the camp boundaries were the SS officers' living quarters, an execution area and an industrial plant owned by the electrical giant Philips. [1]

Vught was the only "official" SS concentration camp in The Netherlands. It was directly under the control of the economic directorate of the SS in Berlin, like the concentration camps in Germany. The building of the barracks complex was paid for with plundered Jewish capital [2]

Sonja, Ro and Ali were immediately separated from their mother, father, brothers and sister never to see them again. I imagine them reaching out to each other in terror with outstretched arms trying to hold on for as long as possible afraid to let go, until an SS Officer finally tears them apart from one another. Whenever I play this scene in my mind, it breaks my heart. What if it was me being separated from my parents, not knowing where they were being taken and if I'd ever see them again? I can't even fathom what this would be like. I would not have been able to let go either.

Sonja was numb with fear, confusion and despair. She and her two sisters were forced into the line for those whose lives would be spared from immediate extermination. Unfortunately, her parents and other siblings were not bestowed with this fate. Instead, they were sent to the Sobibor Death Camp in Poland, an extermination camp where they were murdered in the gas chambers immediately upon arrival. Within this death camp, in operation for only eighteen months, at least 250,000 men, women, and children were murdered. Only 48 Sobibor prisoners survived the war.[3]

Sadly, my family was of the 250,000 who lost their lives and not of the few survivors. As difficult as it is for me to make sense of it, I must believe that this, too, must have been what was *meant to be* for them. I've learned that sometimes in life we can't understand why things happen the way they do, but that we must just try to find a way to accept it and move on. If one chooses to believe that everything in life is *meant to be*, then it must be as true for the bad things that happen as for the good. That is the only way I can make any sense of it. Or maybe, one is not supposed to even try to make sense of what seems so senseless. I'm not sure.

Why did my grandparents have to be killed along with my uncles and aunt? Maybe the Nazis took one look at their ages and physical condition and didn't feel they had enough use for them. Maybe they didn't like the way they looked. Maybe they had some quota to fill of how many they needed to exterminate that day and how many new workers they could bring on. Who knows? The only thing we know is that my mother's life was spared. She was young and healthy looking, and probably looked like she could put in a good day's work. The same would be true for her sisters and that was perhaps why their lives were spared.

I'd like to add here that my father's brother, Louis (commonly known as Weitje), went to The Netherlands from the Dutch East Indies just prior to the war to study agriculture in a place called, Wageningen. He was in the resistance until he got arrested and taken to the Mauthausen Concentration Camp in Austria where he, too, was murdered. Mauthausen was the only Class III designation camp which meant it was the worst camp in the Nazi concentration camp system; it was a punishment camp for resistance fighters who had been accused of sabotage such as my Uncle Weitje and for Allied POWs who were categorized as spies or commandos, Russian POWs who had previously escaped, and German criminals who had been condemned to death.[4] It breaks my heart that I was also deprived of my Uncle Weitje who died much too young like so many of my mother's family in Sobibor.

One of the hardest things about growing up as the daughter of survivors was never knowing any of my grandparents and so few aunts and uncles. Looking at the rare photos, I would often feel a kind of void inside, an emptiness and sense of yearning and longing for all the family members of whom I was so unjustly deprived. I would look into their faces and especially their eyes, wondering not only about them as individuals, but also the generations lost with all the cousins and other relatives I might have had under normal circumstances. What were my grandparents, aunt and uncles like as people? What would my relationships have been like with them? In what ways did I take after them? What might I have learned from them about my parents and family history? What experiences might we have shared and family memories created? As a child I was always secretly jealous of my friends who had large families with grandparents, and lots of aunts, uncles and cousins surrounding them at holidays and family celebrations. I'm not proud of my feelings of jealously, but that is truly how I felt during my teenage years.

To this day, it hurts me deeply to see severed family relationships. Unfortunately, it is often over matters that could be amicably resolved if both parties have the desire to mend differences and are willing to communicate openly and honestly in order to come to a mutual understanding. Maybe this is not always possible, I'm not sure. However, it is a shame when nobody, or only one of those involved makes the effort until it is too late. Too often it is at the end of one's life where a person realizes regrets of the past and wants to make peace. I believe that many of us take our families for granted and sadly don't always share the same level of desire or interest to make the necessary efforts to maintain positive relationships.

Chapter 3

Prisoner in Makassar

After John's ship was captured by the Japanese, one of the enemy cruisers escorted John's ship to the island of Makassar, known today as the provincial capital of South Sulawesi, Indonesia. This, too, was *meant to be,* for although John was taken prisoner, at least he was still alive.

Upon arrival in Makassar, there was total chaos. Japanese officers screamed at the prisoners, counting them over and over in Japanese. John and his fellow POWs didn't understand a word, but the body language of their oppressors spoke volumes. The officers' facial expressions were filled with evil and voices with hate. They pushed and prodded John and the others with sticks and bayonets to keep them moving.

On the way down from the boat, as John passed by the kitchen, he noticed a frying pan sitting on the stove with a cooked steak. When nobody was looking, he bravely picked up the steak and put it inside his shirt. It was the last steak John would eat for the next three and a half years. He remembers wolfing down the steak and enjoying a brief moment of satisfaction. I asked what made him do this and if he even thought about what could have happened if he got caught. He said, *"I didn't think about any risk I was taking. I just did it on impulse."* Thank goodness he did not get caught or I may not be here today. It, too, was *meant to be.*

After disembarking the ship, John and the POWs were forced to march through the city of Makassar carrying big sacs over their shoulders filled with their clothes and other belongings. They had no idea where they were being taken. John remembers seeing the natives lining the streets watching the parade of prisoners.

After walking for what felt like hours in the hot sun, John and the others were so tired that the bags started feeling heavier and heavier, making them increasingly difficult to carry. Slowly, one by one, they began to drop the sacs. John, unable to continue carrying his belongings, had no choice but to also let go of his pack and leave it behind. The natives waited on the sidelines eager to grab the bags full of surprises for them. John looked back at the natives and remembers thinking how they looked like vultures picking at his belongings, free to take whatever they wanted. He turned and kept walking with a deep sense of despair and humiliation. John wondered how much farther he'd have to walk and what was in store for him next.

John arrived at a women's prison where over one hundred prisoners were squeezed into a cell meant to hold only twenty-five to thirty prisoners. He was physically exhausted and dehydrated from the march and was trying to mentally absorb his new surroundings and circumstances. Body to body, barely able to move, he looked around the prison cell and saw that there was only one wooden bucket to serve as a toilet for everyone to share. How could they possibly share only one toilet? How horrible it must have been to live in such dreadful living conditions.

For the first fourteen days John was fed two meals a day consisting of nothing but one small scoop of rice and a flying fish. Because the rice was so constipating, John didn't have a bowel movement for over ten days. This left him in desperate pain and agony. John thought for sure he would die of constipation if he didn't soon get some relief. He didn't know what else to do but pray for help. He was not ready to die and especially in a way he deemed so pitiful.

Soon after, a Japanese sergeant ordered John's friend - a male nurse - to his office to give him a back massage. On the way to the sergeant's office, John's friend passed a storage room where he noticed a shelf filled with large five-pound cans of prunes. On his way back to the cell, when nobody was looking, the brave young man grabbed a can of prunes from the shelf and smuggled it into the prison. He had instantly become a hero in John's eyes for this act of courage. John's prayers were answered.

Now the challenge was to figure out how to open the can without a can opener. John and four of his buddies stood around looking at the can trying to figure out how to open it. John, the most constipated and hence desperate of the bunch, looked around and noticed a tiny nail on the floor. He said to the others, holding the nail up high, with fierce determination and a big grin on his face, *"Look what I just found. I can take this nail and punch holes in the lid. It will take a bit of time, but I can do it and I WILL do it. Just watch me."*

His mates laughed at John and stood by watching as John attempted his idea. They didn't realize John's level of determination. Despite his physical weakness, John managed to find the strength, inspiration and mental fortitude to painstakingly punch little holes side by side in the lid of the can until he was finally able to remove the lid exposing the beautiful prunes inside. It was as if he'd won the lottery. John feasted on handfuls of prunes and the others followed suit. A few hours later, John's stomach began to grumble and eventually he was able to relieve himself giving him back his health, strength and equilibrium. Had his friend not been summoned to the sergeant's office at that moment and happened upon the can of prunes, it is difficult to know what John's fate would have been. If that nail had not been on the floor and caught John's eye and imagination, the can of prunes may still be sitting there. It seems as though once again it was all *meant to be*.

One day, John's friend, a native Ambonese man from the island of Ambon, known for his strong patriotism to former Queen Wilhelmina of The Netherlands, was called to the guard house to remove a photograph of her majesty from the wall. The Japanese officer grabbed the photograph from him, threw it on the floor, and started stomping on it with his boots, laughing and taunting the Ambonese POW. The young man got so mad at the insult and disrespect the officer showed the Queen of The Netherlands, that he punched him in the face in a fit of uncontrolled rage. The officer was stunned and fell hard to the ground.

John watched through the bars of the prison cell as the officer slowly stood up. There was silence. Tension filled the air. Everyone feared for the punishment the young man was surely to receive.

The officer grabbed the young man by his shirt collar and hauled him into to the courtyard where he tied him to a pole. He asked him loudly for all to hear, *"Do you want to be blindfolded for when I shoot you to death as punishment for what you just did to me?"* He replied loud enough for everyone to hear, *"No. I refuse your offer. No blindfold."*

The officer walked back fifteen steps, took his revolver into his hand and started shooting at the man. With every shot, the young POW yelled from the top of his lungs, *"Long live the Queen! Long live the Queen!"*

Infuriated that the prisoner refused to die, the officer went up to the young man and shot him in the head from only an inch away. This was John's first experience of the enemy's capacity for such extreme cruelty. John was deeply angered and saddened by what he witnessed. He quietly grieved the senseless loss of his friend. Although surrounded by fellow prisoners, he remembers never having felt more alone. He was sickened by this tragic event. Any innocence of his youth that might have still existed was now gone forever.

My father remembers how overwhelming it was to come face to face through this incident with the difficult realization of the horrors one human being can inflict upon another. *"What one human being can do to another - I just don't understand it,"* he used to say. This event would haunt him for the rest of his life. As much as he tried, he could not fathom the senselessness of it all. However, he was proud of his friend for at very least not making it so easy for the officer to kill him. John wondered, was this, too, *meant to be?* If yes, why? He learned that there was no answer. The answer was whatever meaning he chose to put to it. Maybe it happened to teach all the other prisoners a lesson of what would happen if they, too, should ever consider hitting or defying an officer. That was the only reason John could think of. He now knew to never defy or lay a hand on an officer no matter how much they mistreat, insult, anger or hurt him.

After two weeks in the overcrowded women's prison, John was transferred to an empty army camp in Makassar located about a fifteen minute walk away. John was in room number 16. There were over one hundred people in the room and everybody had a small space to themselves measuring only three by three one foot tiles. The treatment was much better and the food somewhat improved consisting now of rice, fish and vegetables.

With the extra fiber, John's constipation was not as bad. The enhanced treatment helped him start to feel a little stronger and more hopeful.

Hope was something John quickly learned was a precious commodity. It was not something you could buy, but something you could own any time you wanted a piece of it. He was determined to hold onto hope at all costs because he knew instinctively that without hope he would have nothing.

The little space John occupied was near a window big enough for him to crawl through. The window was about two feet off the floor. Just outside the window, there were big coconut trees full of beautiful coconuts. John would look out at the coconuts and dream of how sweet the coconut milk would be if he could just taste it on his lips and tongue. As there were no guards by the window, John organized a few of the young men to steal some coconuts from the trees. One evening, they each crawled through the window. One of them went to the top of the tree while John and the others waited underneath with a blanket to catch the coconuts before hitting the ground so as not to make noise and risk drawing attention from the nearby guards.

They knew exactly how to open the coconuts without making any noise, and with a wonderful sense of satisfaction, they feasted on every consumable part of the coconuts. John was not afraid. He was happy to be part of the team who shared in his imagination and courage to capture the coconuts and set them free in their mouths and stomachs. He remembers what a delight it was to eat them. John believed it was *meant to be* that they would enjoy the coconuts to know that even in the darkest of times, one can still find moments of light and joy.

One particular day, John looked out the window and saw truckloads of young girls in their school uniforms arriving at the camps. He had no idea what was going on. A POW camp was clearly not a place for young school girls.

Soon after, John was called upon to help build partitions inside nearby elementary schools. He had no idea at first that what he was doing was actually helping to transform these schools into what became known as *military comfort stations*. These were stations where the Japanese soldiers lined up to rape the young innocent girls who were held captive for the sexual pleasure of the soldiers. Many of these girls were picked up off the streets while on their way to school. These girls became known as the *comfort girls* or *comfort women*. Many of them were from occupied countries, including Korea, China and the Philippines, although women from Burma, Thailand, Vietnam, Malaysia, Taiwan (then a Japanese dependency), Indonesia (then the Dutch East Indies), East Timor (then Portuguese Timor) and other Japanese-occupied territories were used for military "comfort stations". A smaller number of women of European origin from the Netherlands and Australia were also involved.[5]

I can't help but think about the poor mothers who sent their girls off to school one morning unaware of the fate awaiting them, never to see their young daughters again. The girls at my father's POW camp, from what he can remember, ranged in age from twelve to maybe fifteen years old. It's hard to imagine how these soldiers and officers derived pleasure by raping poor innocent girls who were resisting them and crying out for help. It is so cruel and inhumane. Do times of war make these behaviors permissible that in times of peace would be considered criminal? It is difficult to comprehend how times of war can change a person's values of respect for another human being, if that is in fact what happened in this case. It is also difficult to accept that the fate of these girls was also *meant to be*. The only purpose it served, in my opinion, was to show the world how cruel and barbaric human beings can be toward one another. Perhaps if we are reminded of this enough, we will one day as a species on this planet be motivated to finally find a better way to live together in peace and harmony. Have we not been reminded of this enough already?

Another one of John's tasks was to put a clean thin cloth over a rope that stretched from one end of the room to the other. The girls were forced to walk naked over this rope after each rape so they could wipe off all the semen from the previous soldier in preparation for the next and the one after that. John watched one girl walk across the towel and then the next and the next, their faces absent of emotion, drained of all humanity. The only thing that these soldiers could not take away from these girls was their will to live. For those who survived, I can only imagine the scars that were left behind physically, mentally, emotionally and spiritually.

John remembers feeling so powerless. It hurt and angered him deeply to hear the girls yelling for help, *"Tolong, tolong,"* and he couldn't do a thing to help them. The loss of freedom as a POW combined with this overwhelming sense of helplessness was devastating to John. He could only hope that these young and impressionable girls would not grow up to think that all men are the same as these barbarians. He wished for them that they would survive and find a man who would love, cherish and respect them in the ways they deserved.

With so much anger and powerlessness, John would do anything he could at every opportunity to take back a sense of control and self-empowerment. The following is one example.

Many of the prisoners were getting sick and often dying from vitamin C deficiency. While working in the inner city cleaning up debris from the bombings, John found three small bags of togarashi in powdered form. Togarashi is a very small hot red chili pepper from Japan known for being extremely rich in potassium, magnesium, iron, vitamin A and vitamin C, having more than double the quantities found in sweeter peppers such as the shishitou. John thought that if he sprinkled some on his rice, it would add extra vitamin C to his diet to keep him from getting sick. Maintaining his health and stamina was one of the ways in which John would take back a sense of control.

John stuffed the little plastic bags of the powdered hot red chili pepper into his shoes to smuggle them into his cell. When he got back to the prison entrance, he passed the guard who ordered him to stop for inspection. The guard checked all of John's pockets and sent him on his way. John kept walking, smiling to himself on the inside with great satisfaction for outsmarting the guard and not getting caught.

Just when he thought the coast was clear, after a few more steps, the guard ordered John to stop and turn around. He called John back and ordered him to take off his shoes. John had no choice but to obey orders. After watching what happened to his Ambonese friend who hit the guard, John knew better than to say a word. His inner smile was quickly replaced by the sick feeling of fear. He instantly broke out into a sweat in anticipation of what the guard would do to him as punishment.

The guard turned the shoes upside down. The bags of togarashi fell to the ground. John did not dare to look up at the guard. He knew he was caught and there was nothing he could do. There was nowhere to hide. John was rightfully terrified knowing that he would be severely reprimanded for this infraction.

As punishment, the guard forced John to swallow the contents of all three bags of the dry hot chili powder without anything to drink. He forced it down John's throat pushing hard with his fingers. John could barely breathe and begged the guard to stop, but the guard was having too much fun watching John suffer. He was not about to stop till every last bit of chili pepper was down John's now burning mouth and throat. John was severely sick for several weeks. The hot pepper burned the lining of his esophagus so badly that it would cause permanent damage and health problems for the rest of his life. If this, too, was *meant to be*, then there must be a reason for it as well.

Let's face it, until this point John had gotten away with successfully stealing the steak from the frying pan and the coconuts from the trees. It gave him such a feeling of satisfaction and invincibility that he didn't hesitate to risk smuggling the hot chili powder given his successful track record. Perhaps what happened in this case was to teach John a lesson that when you take risks in life and try to get away with something, sometimes you'll get away with it and other times you will get caught. This could have been meant as John's reality check that he was not so invincible. The question John learned to ask himself was whether or not after considering the possible consequences of a choice in action he was about to make, is he still willing to take the risk? Is it worth it?

Chapter 4

Prisoner in Nagasaki

In October 1942, John and hundreds of other POWs were taken to the harbor at Makassar where they were put on a freighter called the *Asamah Maruh* headed for Japan. The trip took ten days and was like, *"living in hell,"* he said. The prisoners were crammed into the darkness of the cargo area at the bottom of the ship. There were no toilets and the heat was unbearable. The portholes remained shut for the whole voyage and washing oneself was not permitted. *"Lots of us became very seasick and were throwing up constantly all over the place. There was not very much space to begin with and no air circulation,"* John recalled. They were fed mostly rice with little of anything else.

Upon arrival at the harbor in Nagasaki on October 23, 1942, John got his first taste of winter with cold winds and a temperature of a bitter minus 10 degrees Celsius or 14 degrees Fahrenheit. Unaccustomed to such cold and harsh weather conditions, many of the prisoners got sick with colds and pneumonia. John avoided illness by finding a creative way to stay warm, which was his way of taking back a sense of control over his circumstances.

Here's what happened.

As he disembarked the ship, John noticed a pile of empty cement bags lying in a heap on the side of the walkway. He took a few of the bags, ripped holes in them with his fingers, put his head and arms through the holes, and layered the bags over his coat to keep the cold out. I marvel at how resourceful he was to think of doing something so clever. He had no control over the weather. However, what he did have control over was his imagination and ability to act on it. When he saw the cement bags that the others passed by, he instantly saw an opportunity. He envisioned himself wearing these bags for protection from the cold. He knew he had to act quickly as he did not have the luxury of time on his side. He watched others die from the cold while he managed to survive, yet again. It was by miracle and might that were all *meant to be.*

John and the remaining POWs were marched to the famous Fukuoka II, a wooden camp with a guardhouse and a high barbed wire fence all around it. Again they were yelled at, poked and prodded, counted and re-counted and then searched. Everything sharp was taken away. The camp was built in a U-form with eighteen rooms on each side and in the connecting rounded part were the washrooms and kitchen. There were fifty-two POWs maximum in each room. There were bunk beds on each side of the room, two rows of thirteen. John was in room 14. He was given an identification number printed on a band of cloth that he was forced to sew on all his clothes: it was N°· 620.[6]

After a few days of rest, dysentery broke out among the prisoners. Many of those afflicted became dehydrated very quickly. They were given opium drops to stop the diarrhea. Unfortunately, they frequently did not make it to the toilets in time, as the waiting lines became longer and longer every day.

Tragically, many died during the first period in this camp. John was extremely grateful for somehow managing to escape this first round of dysentery.

John's first job in Japan was as a slave laborer in the shipyards. When it came time to report for work duty, John learned that they needed drillers, cleaners and welders. John chose to be a cleaner which he discovered meant sitting in front of big heaps of dirt collected off the ships that were being built and retrieving all the nuts and bolts and other metal objects for cleaning and re-use.

There was little supervision with the guards stationed a fair distance away. There was only a wharf foreman in charge. The cold weather made the job very difficult, especially without gloves. As a result, John's fingers became badly swollen. The noise of working at the shipyards was unbearable and John was worried he might lose his hearing. As a result, he was desperate for some relief from the constant loudness surrounding him, but didn't know what to do. Just then he saw some newspapers nearby. When nobody was looking, John snatched a newspaper and tore off two little pieces. He put them in his mouth to wet them and then cleverly put a piece of wet newspaper in each of his ears for relief. With the wet newspaper acting as earplugs, John managed to drown out enough of the sound to make it a little more bearable. I truly believe that this kind of imagination and resourcefulness were keys to his ultimate survival and well-being. As he would tell you, the newspapers were there for a reason. It was *meant to be* that he would find them and think to turn them into ear plugs to save his hearing.

One bitter cold afternoon, John and a friend snuck under one of the ships to warm up by the switch fire used to heat up the rivets. They were only planning to get a few short moments of reprieve from the cold, but those few moments were a few too many. The guard came by unexpectedly and caught them hiding. He was infuriated that they were not busy working. He called them out from under the ship and ordered them to hold themselves in a push up position on the ground. John and his friend took their positions. The guard sharply warned them that if he saw their bodies sag in the slightest, he would give them a beating so hard they would never forget. To raise the stakes even higher, the guard put a little fire underneath their bellies. If John's body lowered, he would get burned by the fire. John did all he could to keep the push up position without bending, but as his strength got the better of him, his body began to sag. The guard beat him repeatedly on his back and bottom with the butt of his gun, showing no mercy whatsoever. John could hear the guard laughing with every strike. John could hardly sit for over a week from the painful bruising on his backside that faded from black and blue to purple and grey. He had to go to the infirmary to have his belly treated for slight burns as well. His stomach muscles hurt for weeks afterwards. I remember him saying, *"I wish I could block the sound of the guard's laughter from my memory."* By this time, John had already been physically abused on many occasions. However, he never gave up his will to live and determination to keep going. He had every reason to give up hope, but instead, with every torture or beating, he stayed strong, confident and trusting that the war would soon end and he would somehow come out of it alive. As long as he could stay healthy and be useful to his enemy, he knew he could survive.

After the constant suffering from the cold, John was envious of the riveters who used a little coal stove to heat up the rivets before installing them on the steel plates of the ships. The heat from the stove helped them stay warm. He knew that before the weather turned even colder, he would have to find a way to keep warmer to stay healthy and survive. The cost of getting sick was too high, as John knew that prisoners who got sick only received half a ration of food. John could not afford to lose any more weight. He decided that as soon as they needed more welders, he would quickly volunteer. It was a lucky break, or perhaps *meant to be,* that he just happened to have learned how to weld at the technical school back home before the war. All he cared about was receiving his welding outfit to keep warm, which included a canvas jacket and trousers plus a welding helmet and mask.

When they were finally looking for volunteers, John stepped up and was ordered to make a test piece to prove his skills. As John was out of practice, having not done any welding since his schooling, he did not want to take any chances of not getting the job. As this was too important and there was no room for error, he knew he had to find a way to fool the inspector. In glancing down on the floor, John happened to notice two pieces of metal that were already perfectly welded together. Just before the foreman came for inspection, John quickly heated up the welded piece with an acetylene burner to make it look like it was freshly welded. The foreman was very impressed with the quality of John's work and the next day John received his welding outfit that would help him stay warm. Mission accomplished. Once again it was a miracle that he happened to find the welded piece on the floor at exactly the right moment and had the imagination to act on using it to fool the inspector. It was another example of *meant to be.*

As the weather turned colder, John was glad to have his canvas outfit to keep warm and increase his chances for survival. If he could only manage to stay healthy, then he would be one step closer to getting out alive.

John worked in the snow and cold of winter wearing shoes three to four sizes too big. Unfortunately, they had no sizes for the shorter men like John because all the Americans, Dutch and other prisoners were typically much taller with bigger size feet.

However, what seemed like a problem at first, turned out to be a blessing in disguise.

Here's what happened.

John needed a way to stop his shoes from falling off his feet when he walked. Using his imagination yet again, an idea came to him to fill the front end of his shoes with straw so that his heels would stay in place and the shoes wouldn't keep slipping off. One day, while a crane was moving the heavy metal plates from the boat with big cables, one cable got loose. Without warning, the huge metal plate came falling down, and within a split second landed precisely on the toes of John's right foot, precisely where he had just finished stuffing the straw into his shoes. If he didn't have the straw in his shoes, his toes would have been sheared off instantly, and if the heavy metal plate had fallen a few more inches to the right, it would have landed on his head killing him instantaneously. John looked down, slid his foot out from the shoe and walked away unharmed. He then looked up to God, or whatever you want to call the force that was looking after him, in gratitude for yet another miracle that proved to save his life. It was *meant to be*.

Another day, John stood looking over the edge of the ship. The surrounding noise of the riveting was so loud that he couldn't hear a thing. Then unbeknownst to John, a counter weight attached to a cable slipped causing the weight to come hurling down towards him. Everybody was yelling to him in a panic to get out of the way, but he couldn't hear their warnings due to all the noise. John was totally oblivious. As the weight came down, it grazed the side of John's cap. At that very instant, the crane operator was able to stop the cable and fall of the weight just before it crushed John's outstretched hand. In complete awe and astonishment, everyone watched as John simply pushed the weight away with his hand and re-adjusted his hat. Had he been standing an inch or two further to the right, it would have landed on his head and killed him. One millionth of a second more and John would have surely lost his hand. All his friends laughed with relief. John was in shock and disbelief. When it finally sank in how narrowly he escaped death and injury, he looked up to God with gratitude for saving his hand and once again sparing his life. After being spared so many times and in such extraordinary ways, John knew better than to believe that it was simply random luck or another coincidence. He knew in his heart that it was another one of those miracles that was simply *meant to be*.

John had managed to avoid the outbreaks of dysentery for so long, but in early 1943 it was finally his turn. He lost a lot of weight and remembers being so thin that he could count his ribs. The doctor gave him opium drops to stop the outflow of diarrhea. He was very grateful for having survived it, as many died from this terrible disease.

I have seen many photographs of POWs in the Japanese prison camps looking like skin and bone. They were completely emaciated from starvation and sickness. Having only known my father in times of health and even slightly overweight, it is very difficult for me to picture him so severely sick, malnourished and underweight. I am very grateful to whatever forces allowed him to pull through, including the miracles of his own will and might.

John remembers how he and his mates got baths once every ten days in a cement pool about 12 x 15 ft. The idea was to be the first to get there and wash up as soon as possible. Even if the water was boiling hot, it was clean only for the first groups in line which were organized according to room number. By the time it was the last room's turn, the water would be black. To make things fair, the guards rotated the schedule so that every time a different room would be the first in line. On those occasions, when everyone was naked waiting their turn, John remembers seeing everyone's ribs and bones sticking out, as well as the bites of bedbugs and lice which had left welts and marks all over their bodies. Nonetheless, John was grateful to at least feel clean once every ten days.

That winter was very hard on John. The days were short and he wondered how much longer his prison time would last. He was starting to doubt how much longer he could keep on going now that he lost so much weight and his health had deteriorated so drastically due to the dysentery and malnutrition. Sometimes he couldn't help but feel down. During those dark moments of despair, rather than isolate himself, John would seek out his friends. They would sit around together as a group and talk about willpower and trust in God, believing that God would take care of everything. He remembers how they supported one another, sharing stories about their lives before the war, what the future might bring and their plans for when they would regain their freedom. [6]

I truly believe that the support these young men gave to one another was invaluable in their ability to hold onto hope and cope with their suffering. What amazes me is that regardless of their differences in religious beliefs - my father was Jewish and the others were Christian, Catholic and Muslim - they all shared the same sense of faith and trust in God that somehow they would get through their time of captivity and live in freedom again one day. They all got along and there was no hate toward each other because of their religious differences.

Chapter 5

Sonja in Camp Vught

While John suffered the camps at Makassar and Nagasaki, Sonja was put to slave labor at the Philips Company industrial plant in camp Vught. Philips employed some twelve-hundred Jewish and non-Jewish prisoners to make radio equipment and torches. This group of prisoners were known as the *Philips Kommando* or *"Philips Group,"* as my mother called it. For the prisoners of Vught, a job with Philips meant delayed deportation.[7]

Sonja did not fully realize at the time how being selected for slave labor in the Philips Kommando would help to save her life.

My mother did not talk much about her time in the concentration camps, but there are a few remarkable stories that she shared. There's one story from her time with the Philips Group that I will always remember. It is a strong example of the cruel Nazi mindset and courage that my mother exemplified in the face of their evil.

Here's what happened.

One day, while working on the radio assembly line, a Nazi guard started shouting at my mother in front of everyone, accusing her of sabotaging one of the radios. Knowing that she absolutely did not and would not ever do such a thing, my mother stood up to the Nazi and fearlessly proclaimed her innocence.

Determined to scare her into confessing to the crime, the Nazi pointed his shotgun within inches of her face, and with a menacing look in his eyes yelled at her, *"I know you did it so just admit to me that you did it or I will shoot you dead right here and now."* Everyone stopped what they were doing to watch and listen to what would happen next. She remembers her sisters telling her how they broke out in a sweat of fear, terrified that Sonja would be shot to death before their eyes.

Refusing to give in, Sonja bravely stood her ground. With the gun still inches from her face, she replied with fire in her eyes and her head held high, *"I didn't do it. If you want to shoot me, then shoot me, but I will tell you again that it wasn't me. I didn't do it."*

The Nazi did all he could to get Sonja to admit to her guilt, but no matter how loud he yelled and close he put that shotgun to her face, she refused to back down. *"He was not going to get me,"* she told me.

Finally, the Nazi swiftly turned around with the shotgun and shot the girl who he knew sabotaged the radio all along. He shot her in the head, point blank. She collapsed to the ground to her immediate death. Laughing, he turned to Sonja and said, *"I just wanted to see how far I could push you."* For him, it appeared to all be a game. He was simply having fun.

In shock, with her feet frozen to the ground, Sonja knew better than to let the Nazi see how much she was shaking inside from the whole ordeal. When it was all said and done, the Nazi motioned to Sonja and everyone else to get back to work. It was then business as usual.

When I reflect on this story, it boggles my mind how much strength and courage it took for my mother, just a teenager at the time, to stand up to this evil Nazi. If she would have shown her fear, or given in to his pushing her, she believed wholeheartedly that he would have shot her dead. He could have chosen to shoot her just for the fun of it, but he let her live. Once again her life was spared. Was it just luck, or was it *meant to be*? I choose to believe that it was *meant to be* and an incredible example of the powerful combination of God's miracles, and her own might to stand up to the Nazi.

One Friday night, Sonja decided to light the Shabbat candles and sing the prayers over them. I'm not sure exactly how she lit the candles. I read on the Internet of another story where a girl made two little candles from the margarine she saved and did not eat, and took some threads from the bottom of her dress and lit them.[8] Perhaps my mother did the same or something similar. Regardless of how she lit the candles, the fact that she sung the prayers out loud for everyone to hear matters more than anything. It was a very brave act indeed. Everyone was nervous for her at first and begged her not to do it for fear she would be punished or killed. She refused to stop. She remembered how singing the prayers with her whole heart and soul lifted her spirit and gave her strength while quickly bringing a few moments of reprieve, hope and light to the others where so much darkness loomed.

A Nazi guard was seen outside the window listening the whole time. His appreciation of such a beautiful singing voice overtook his hatred and sense of duty for that short period of time. When she was finished singing, he came inside and said to her, *"You're lucky you have such a fine singing voice or I would have had to exterminate you."*

Once again, it is amazing to me that my mother had the courage to do such a thing. For her, Friday night was sacred. While growing up, my mother always lit the Shabbat candles, without fail. My father said the blessings over the freshly baked Challah breads and cup of sweet kosher wine. It was tradition. My mother always cherished those special times which now serve as special memories for me, too. My mother followed the traditions as it was simply a part of who she was. From her not cowering to the Nazi who accused her of sabotage to her bravely singing the Shabbat prayers, clearly my mother was not afraid to die. My belief is that she would have rather died than not honor her true self and do what she believed was right in her heart. It is difficult for me to have anything less than the utmost respect for her strength and bravery.

Chapter 6

Life in Auschwitz

On June 7, 1943, my mother and her sisters were taken from their barrack and stuffed onto an overcrowded cattle car. Little did they know that the train was headed for the infamous Auschwitz concentration and death camp. She remembers how there were so many men, women and children all crammed in together that she could barely breathe or move. She was desperately thirsty, hungry and frightened beyond words. The barrack she lived in at Vught had become her new home. Although the conditions were poor, she at least knew what to expect. Now she was being forced to face the unknown once again.

The discomfort, hunger, thirst and feelings of suffocation with the lack of air and circulation were beyond imagination. Adults and children alike had no choice but to urinate and defecate standing up. The resulting stench must have been unbearable.

After surviving such a wretched train ride, they finally arrived at Auschwitz. Built by the Nazis as both a concentration and death camp, Auschwitz was the largest and most notorious of the Nazi's camps and the most streamlined mass killing center ever created. It was at Auschwitz that 1.1 million people were murdered, mostly Jews. Auschwitz has become a symbol of death, the Holocaust, and the destruction of European Jewry. [9] Living conditions were brutal, and many of those not killed in the gas chambers died of starvation, forced labor, infectious diseases, individual executions, and medical experiments. [10]

She was ordered to leave all her belongings on board and gather with the others upon the railway platform, known as "the ramp." An SS officer ordered each individual into one of two lines, one for those who would be put to death and the other for slave labor.[11]

Sonja was once again spared from the death line and sent to the right for hard labor at Auschwitz II (Birkenau). Auschwitz II (or "Birkenau") was completed in early 1942. Birkenau was built approximately 1.9 miles (3 km) away from Auschwitz I and was the real killing center of the Auschwitz death camp. It was in Birkenau where the dreaded selections were carried out on the ramp and where the sophisticated and camouflaged gas chambers laid in waiting. Birkenau, much larger than Auschwitz I, housed the most prisoners and included areas for women and Gypsies. [12]

Sonja was immediately lined up for the dehumanizing process designed to remove any remnants of human dignity or personal identity. First she was stripped of her clothing and any remaining personal belongings. Then her hair was shaved till she was completely bald. She remembers watching helplessly as her hair fell to the ground, much like when her mother shaved Sonja's head due to lice. She was given a striped prison uniform and a pair of shoes that were the wrong size. The final dehumanizing step was being registered and tattooed with a number on her left arm just like the branding of a cow. Sonja had already lost her freedom, her belongings, her home, her family and now she would lose her name and identity, too. She would be known as number 78491, the ultimate of dehumanization. However, I can remember my mother telling me how she already started saying to herself then, *"They can do whatever they want to me, but I will never let them get me. They will never have my soul."* She was determined to never lose her will to live.

In the morning, Sonja was assembled outside with the other prisoners to stand for hours at roll call (Appell) where everyone was to be counted. She didn't understand what was happening and just followed orders feeling powerless and frightened by the harsh tones of the Nazis' evil voices.

Suddenly, Sonja noticed a mother and her two identical twin daughters standing side by side. The officer grabbed the twins and took them away from the mother. Sonja was mortified. She was overwhelmed with intense compassion for the poor mother who was screaming and crying out in terror as she refused to release her little girls from her tight hold. Careful not to draw unwanted attention, Sonja didn't dare say a word or let her true emotions show. She fought hard to keep her face empty of expression and tears at bay.

Sonja watched the officer shoot the mother in the head for trying to stop him from grabbing her precious little girls. She found out later that the twins were taken to the experimental block where Dr. Josef Mengele, nicknamed *The Angel Of Death*, and the other Nazi doctors at the death camps tortured men, women and children and did medical experiments of unspeakable horror during the Holocaust. At Auschwitz, Josef Mengele did a number of medical experiments using twins. These twins, as young as five years of age, were usually murdered after the experiment was over and their bodies dissected. Mengele injected chemicals into the eyes of the children in an attempt to change their eye color. He carried out twin-to-twin transfusions, stitched twins together, castrated or sterilized twins. Many twins had limbs and organs removed in macabre surgical procedures, performed without using an anesthetic.[13] Sonja was deeply traumatized by what she had witnessed. She felt so helpless and powerless in the same way that John must have felt when he could hear the innocent comfort girls screaming out for help, unable to do a thing to help them.

After roll call, Sonja and a group of other prisoners were marched to the railroad where she worked for twelve hour days building railways. She attributed much of the pain in her back that would plague her for the rest of her life to those back-breaking days of hard physical labor.

Meal times in the camp were the most important event of each day. After morning roll call, the prisoners would be given their morning 'meal' – imitation coffee or herbal 'tea'. For lunch prisoners would be given a litre of watery soup. If they were lucky, they might find a piece of turnip or potato peel.[14] I know my mother had her fill of turnips because I can still remember her saying on more than one occasion, *"Turnips we will never eat in this house. I have eaten enough turnips for a lifetime and never want to see another one again."* In the evening prisoners would be given a piece of black bread weighing 300 grams, together with a tiny piece of sausage or margarine, marmalade or cheese. Because the bread was also supposed to last the prisoners for the morning, they would try to hide it on their person whilst they slept.

The lack of food, poor diet and hard labor caused the prisoners to suffer from starvation sickness. They lost weight and muscle tissue and many thousands died. Others who became too weak to work were then murdered in the gas chambers.

The appalling conditions in the camp were made worse by the fact that Auschwitz-Birkenau had been built on a swamp. The barracks were often damp. Lice and rats were everywhere. As a result, epidemics of contagious diseases were frequent.[15]

Sonja knew she had to stay strong to withstand all the hardships. In addition to the dreadful living conditions, other reasons for people dying of epidemics and contagious diseases were due to the fouling of straw and straw mattresses by prisoners suffering from diarrhea. This made difficult living conditions even worse. More than seven hundred people were assigned to each barrack, although in practice the figure was sometimes higher. These barracks lacked any true heating. A constant shortage of water for washing, and the lack of suitable sanitary facilities, aggravated the situation.[16]

It is unbelievable to me how my mother, or anyone for that matter, was able to survive the terrible living conditions and epidemics. I truly believe that what allowed them to pull through was their personal might and perseverance combined with God's grace and miracles. It was surely *meant to be* that my mother had the strength in body and spirit to keep on going despite all her suffering.

After hours of hard physical labor, Sonja and the prisoners were marched back to camp for another roll call. Sonja watched people drop to their death of exhaustion and starvation. She saw others shot to death if they were caught stopping to simply catch their breath. She tried not to look knowing she had to remain strong and just keep working, no matter what. She continued to work and push herself to her limits despite the pain, exhaustion, hunger and thirst. With determination and satisfaction, Sonja mumbled to herself over and over the mantra that kept her going, *"Hitler will never get me. Hitler will never get me."*

One morning, while assembled outside with the other prisoners at daily roll call to be counted, Sonja saw a new mother with identical twin daughters who were maybe five or six years old. As expected, the girls stood close by their mother's side. Sonja instantly remembered what happened to the twins last time and was compelled to do whatever she could to not let it happen again. She could not bear it.

With amazing nerve, while the SS officer was at the other end of the line with his back to her, Sonja warned the mother to separate the girls. In a desperate whisper, she beseeched the mother to make sure her daughters stand far away from each other so the officer doesn't take notice of them. Sonja told the mother how horrible things would be done to her daughters, and they might even be killed if she didn't listen to her immediately. The mother, in disbelief, automatically resisted Sonja's pleading. How could a mother separate her girls from her and from each other? She refused to take such drastic measures.

Afraid for the horrific fate of the little girls, Sonja grabbed one of them and placed her in the back row far enough away from the identical sister in the hopes that the SS officer wouldn't notice. She told the girl not to make a sound and prayed the girl, her mother and sister would remain silent. Sonja rushed back to her place just in time without the officer noticing. Everyone watched and knew what she was doing, but thankfully nobody reacted or said a word. The officer didn't see a thing. At the first safe opportunity, Sonja and the mother snuck a look at each other of relief and gratitude. The mother would be forever indebted to Sonja for bravely saving her little girls.

Where did my mother find the courage to do such a thing? If my mother didn't do exactly what she did, those twins would in all likelihood have suffered unimaginable pain and suffering and possibly death. When I asked my mother about it, she said, *"I don't remember thinking about whether or not to do it. It was a choice I had to make, something I had to do."* The first time it happened and she saw the twins taken away from their mother, she did not know what was happening, so was unable to help. This time was different. She now knew what their fate would likely be, and she would rather have died than allow it to happen again when she knew she had the power to save them. Complacency was not a viable option for her this time, as she saw an opportunity to act and simply seized it. Once again my mother had an angel looking over her. It was *meant to be* that she would have the nerve to perform such an act of courage and a miracle that the SS Officer did not catch her. It was *meant to be* for those little girls and their mother to survive.

One day, Sonja was taken to the gas chamber. Standing in the crowded line with hundreds of others, awaiting her death, she watched the smoke coming out of the smoke stack knowing it was the ashes of her *"brothers and sisters,"* as she would say. She remembers thinking to herself how she will never be able to live her dream of being married and raising a family of her own. The line began to move forward and Sonja was now inside the gas chamber. She knew her time had come and there was nowhere to escape, nothing she could do but surrender to her circumstances.

All of a sudden, an officer yelled in anger, *"You are all very lucky. The gas has run out."* He ordered Sonja and the rest of the prisoners back to the barracks at once. Sonja was numb with disbelief at her good fortune. She had managed to circumvent death once again. It was clearly not her time to die. The gas running out was a miracle that was surely *meant to be.*

While waiting for the guards to refill the gas, Sonja was put on a train for transport to yet another unknown destination, a new concentration camp. She remembers crying intense tears of relief that her life was spared mixed with fear for what was next to come.

What is even more miraculous is that the same fate happened two more times during the course of the eleven camps where she was held in captivity. This means that on three separate occasions she was taken to the gas chambers and each time there was either a malfunction with the gas supply, or they had gassed so many prisoners that particular day that by the time it was my mother's turn, they had run out of gas. Call it what you will, but as far as I'm concerned it was not her time to die. There was still much purpose left for her life. Each time was another miracle of fate that was surely *meant to be.*

Sonja and her sisters were taken to Reichenbach where they worked for the Telefunken electronics company. They lived in the concentration camp two miles South of Reichenbach in the municipality of Langenbielau.[17] Telefunken adopted the Philips Kommando prisoners since they would require less training and already proved to be good workers. As long as she belonged to this group, she had value as a skilled worker. Sonja knew to work this to her advantage and ensured that she always did good quality work.

A typical day for Sonja at Reichenbach would include a two mile walk from the camp to the factory, working a twelve hour shift on her feet and then the walk back. By the end of each day, Sonja was exhausted, with unbearable pain in her back, legs and feet from standing all day. Every day she would renew her vow to never give in to the pain. She was determined to never give up staying true to her mantra, *"Hitler will never get me".*

Chapter 7

John in the Coal Mines

Three months before the war ended, John was transferred from the shipyards to work in the coal mines located about fifteen to twenty kilometers from Nagasaki. John knew that because coal mine workers would get so dirty, they could take showers daily as opposed to the one shower he was allowed every ten days while working in the shipyard. For this reason and this reason only, John happily volunteered to work in the coal mines. He had no idea at the time how this decision would ultimately save his life.

Here's what happened.

John and the other POWs being transferred were put on a train to the nearby coal mine camp. The windows on the train were tightly shut. They all sat close together like sardines in a can. There was hardly any room for John to maneuver himself to the toilets. He just prayed he would not need to use one. When he arrived at the camp, the sight was daunting. The camp looked horrible from the outside. He never worked in a coal mine before and had no idea what was in store for him. [18]

John was used to the bed bugs and lice from his camp at the shipyards, but nothing prepared him for what it was like in the coal mines. He was constantly being bitten. When everybody surfaced from the mines, they'd remove all their clothing to find their long underwear full of bugs and lice. He remembers turning to the wall behind his bed and seeing all the streaks of blood from the bugs he killed with his shoes. After a short while of dealing with the excessive bed bugs, lice and terrible living conditions, John told a friend that maybe he'd made a mistake transferring to the coal mines, after all. He couldn't imagine how much worse it could possibly get.

It was also much colder in the mines than John expected. In the morning he would go down by a little train at least 2000 feet below ground. He walked down in what he described as, *"those big black holes"* with the big mining lamp on top of his head and a big pick to pick the coal. He'd regularly have to step over cracks in the earth where he looked down unable to see the bottom. I couldn't even imagine how scary this must have been and how careful he would have to be with every step.

Then there were the explosions. The Japanese made holes in which they'd place dynamite to blow up and shatter the coal. John and the prisoners would then be forced to shovel the shattered coal into little wagons. This was his routine from morning till night. It was hard, back breaking labor that left him physically exhausted by the end of each day. He remembers not seeing daylight until the weekend, as he left very early in the morning when it was still dark, and it was already dark when the work day was over.

Malnutrition was the norm in the camp. Rations were very meagre due to the severe food shortages in wartime Japan. John was forced to endure near-starvation conditions as the closing days of the war approached. Despite the insufficient food rations, John was still expected to meet the demands of his work in the coal mine. It was a very difficult and desperate time.

John remembers how when he heard about the planes flying over to bomb Tokyo or other places many times a day, the POWs all felt that freedom could not be far off. This gave them hope that the war would soon end, but they did not want to get their hopes up too high and expect too much.[19] They just continued to pray for freedom, and that their bodies would somehow stay healthy and strong enough to support them.

Chapter 8

Free at Last for John

In the spring of 1945, John and his mates heard that Germany had surrendered. This good news increased their hope that maybe Japan would surrender soon, too. On August 9th, John and his fellow POWs heard a loud explosion. They thought it was another ammunition dump that had been bombed. In the evening when they came up from the mines, they saw a red glow in the distance. That's when they realized something major had happened. This was no ordinary ammunition bombing. He later learned that it was the atomic bomb that the Americans had dropped on Nagasaki to end the war.

On August 15th, John noticed the Japanese soldiers listening to the radio with long faces of defeat. There were no more sounds of air raid sirens, and the night shift did not have to go to work. The tension in the camp was mounting. John and his fellow POWs sensed that this was the end of the war.[20]

The Japanese soldiers were informed by their officers that the Emperor had decided to end the war. John and the other prisoners were free at last.

John and all his mates were thrilled when they saw the B29 airplanes come flying overhead dropping big oil drums filled with canned food, chocolate and cigarettes. *"The airplanes flew so low, it was incredible. We were singing and dancing. There was a jubilant feeling of freedom in the air. We were drunk on life without a drop of alcohol,"* he told me with a big smile on his face.

John's friend, the male nurse who got him the prunes early on, ordered all the now ex-POWs to not touch the food until he had a chance to distribute the proper portions. Not surprisingly, after being deprived of food for so long, not all the men would listen. John watched many of his buddies overindulge on chocolate and canned food. After seeing how their feet swelled up as their bodies were no longer used to so much food all at once, John listened wisely to his friend and controlled himself to be rationed slowly.

The Americans came on land to rescue them and on September 18th, the free ex-POWs left the camp and were taken by train to Nagasaki. This time every window was open. John remembers how they yelled at the farmers in the fields with excitement. They chewed gum and smoked the best of cigarettes.

The train arrived in Nagasaki where the bomb was dropped only a month prior. It took about forty minutes to get to the main station where the American Red Cross was waiting for them. John recalls the silence when they saw the damage. He could only make out a few streets and remnants of concrete buildings. Everything was burnt. The city was no more. The burning smell still lingered and it seemed that the shadows of the dead were everywhere. Only the clicking of the wheels of the train was heard as John travelled through this mass grave. [21]

It was only after witnessing the devastation that John could fully grasp his good fortune to have been underground when the bomb exploded. Had he still been working in the shipyards when the bomb exploded, he would likely not have survived. Was this just another amazing coincidence? I think not. My father's life was not meant to come to such a premature end. Why was his life spared and not the others? That is a question I cannot answer. That is part of the essence of this incredible miracle that was surely *meant to be.*

From Nagasaki, John and the others continued on to Okinawa where they were put on a plane to Manila. They stayed in Manila for three months to recuperate. Although John received the medical attention he needed, the doctors didn't know what to do for his scarred and damaged esophagus from the severe punishment of swallowing the hot chili powder.

During that time, John started putting meat back on his bones and regaining his physical strength. However, there was no psychiatric help like there is for soldiers today. As a result, he watched a lot of his buddies struggle mentally to cope with what was likely Post Traumatic Stress Syndrome.

While in Manila, another miracle happened for John. Some incredible force was once again at play when by chance he met a sergeant who he discovered through conversation just happened to also be Jewish. John mentioned that he was not brought up religious and was curious to learn more about the beliefs and customs of his people. The sergeant said to John, *"Why don't you join the Jewish youth group here in Manila? It's called Habonim."* John joined the youth group which he would tell you played a big role in his ability to cope mentally and spiritually with his difficult transition from captivity to liberty. He delighted in meeting young people who were close to his own age. He remembers enjoying playing games and cards with them, reveling in the immense freedom of swimming in the ocean and how wonderful it was to lie leisurely on the beach without a care in the world. He relished their company and appreciated the ability to laugh again.

By surrounding himself with positive people close to his own age, he regained the ability to experience the feeling of true joy.

This enabled John to better cope with the adjustment to his newly found freedom versus many of his friends who instead chose to isolate themselves.

This is something very powerful to consider. Many times when faced with adversity and stressful situations, there is a tendency to keep it to ourselves, believing that we must suffer and solve our problems alone. Feeling isolated, we don't realize that reaching out to others and surrounding ourselves with joyful people can actually help us heal and overcome, especially if those others are positive people who can help us feel a sense of safety and belonging.

It was through the youth group that John met a girl named Margo. He went out with her a few times and quickly became smitten by her. The relationship came to an abrupt end when she went back to the United States to finish her education. John never heard from her again until fate brought them together some sixty years later. It was truly a miracle and clearly another inspiring example of something that was surely *meant to be*.

Here's what happened.

Imagine sixty years after the war, in 2005, a year after my mother's passing, my father was being interviewed over the telephone on live radio in Israel. The radio station was interviewing former POWs like my dad. When the host announced the next guest as John Franken, a woman suddenly yelled out in disbelief from the background, *"Johnny Franken? Johnny Franken?"* It was Margo who recognized him by name. She was living in Israel and being interviewed live in the studio. My dad could hardly believe his ears. They both talked excitedly to each other on live radio and we heard later that all of Israel was listening and wondering what was going to happen to the two of them. They exchanged contact information and started writing to each other by email. My father would tell you that this was not a coincidence. As far as he's concerned this was another source of proof that everything in life is *meant to be*. He saw no other way to explain how the timing was so perfect for her to still be in the studio while the host introduced my dad. She could have just left the studio or gone to the washroom. She could have forgotten his name. There are so many things that happened that were so perfectly aligned for the two of them to rekindle their relationship.

After three months in Manila, John was asleep in his hammock one night when an officer said to him and a few others, *"Whoever is interested in going to Australia, report to me."* Without blinking an eye and fearless as ever, John rolled up his hammock and said to the officer, *"Here I am. I am ready to go."* John was eager to go to Australia so he could finally finish his aircraft mechanic training. He was taken by plane to Sydney the next day.

After approximately eight months in Sydney, John went to The Netherlands where he finished the remainder of his ten-year Navy contract. He stopped first in Indonesia to find his mother. Sadly, John learned that his mother died in a Japanese internment camp.

Upon his return to The Netherlands, John managed to reunite with his brothers Paul, Albert and Joop as well as Mrs. Van der Velde. Mr. Van der Velde had sadly also died in the war. If you'll remember, it was Mr. Van der Velde who performed the wedding ceremony for my Uncle Paul and his wife in the pre-wartime Dutch East Indies.

John learned that his brother Weitje had died in Mauthausen and that Albert, Paul and Joop had been captured by the Japanese and put to slave labor building the infamous Burma

Railway, also known as the Death Railway, the Burma-Siam Railway, the Thailand–Burma Railway and similar names. It was a 415 kilometer (258 mi) railway between Bangkok, Thailand, and Rangoon, Burma (now Yangon, Myanmar), built by the Empire of Japan in 1943, to support its forces in the Burma campaign of World War II. Forced labor was used in its construction. About 12,399 Allied POWs died as a direct result of the project. The dead POWs included 6,318 British personnel, 2,815 Australians, 2,490 Dutch, about 356 Americans, and about 20 POWs from other British Commonwealth countries (the Indian Empire, New Zealand and Canada).[22]

John's brother Joop

Joop and Paul were liberated at the end of the war. However, Albert's story of survival is quite remarkable. At one point during the war when Albert was too sick to work due to the high fevers of malaria attacks, a Japanese officer threw him into the swamps to die. Too weak and sick to climb his way out of the swamps, he could see no way of coming out of this predicament alive. Then suddenly, when his hope was as depleted as his strength, a native Thai girl found him. She dragged him out of the swamp and nursed him back to life. Like a fairy tale, the two fell in love, married and moved to The Netherlands to live happily ever after.

Uncle Albert and Tante Nittje

What an incredible miracle of fate that just as Albert was getting ready to die, this young girl would happen to find him and nurse him back to life. If she had arrived much later, he would likely have already been dead and there would have been nothing she could do to help. This, too, was *meant to be*.

I will always remember my Uncle Albert and Tante Nittje who I am so glad to have known and visited in The Netherlands on many occasions in my youth. Post-war, Albert worked in the army hospital as a male nurse for emergency care. He died on April 16, 1970 of a heart attack. Joop, John's oldest brother, became a guard at a military base in The Netherlands and died on October 27, 1965 of a stroke.

After the war, my Uncle Paul moved to Canada where he had his own shop working as an optician. He died in Montreal on May 30, 1970, also of a heart attack. I'm so grateful to have known him when I was a little girl, even for a brief time. Unfortunately, Uncle Joop died before I ever had the chance of meeting him.

In December 1950, John was discharged from the Navy. With no jobs available for aircraft mechanics, John took a job in a paint factory. In October 1951, John saw a big ad in the newspaper promoting job openings in the aircraft industry in Montreal, Canada. This ad would change the course of his life. A company called Canadair was building aircrafts for the war in Korea and they needed mechanics. John took a chance and went to Montreal with no job and nothing but fifty dollars in his pocket and a heart full of hope.

With fierce determination, he waited in the employment office at Canadair all day every day for four straight days till someone finally came down and said, *"I need an inspector for parts. Anyone qualified and interested?"* John stood up, stepped forward and said he was interested and ready to start immediately.

I think about this story and wonder what the staff in the employment office were thinking of this strange man who would sit there all day just waiting for a job. They could have asked him to leave, but they didn't. Each day when he returned, I can only imagine them admiring his perseverance which clearly paid off in the end. John was thrilled to get a steady job in his field of expertise and eager to make a new life as a proud Canadian citizen.

Chapter 9

Free at Last for Sonja

In February 1945, Sonja and her sisters were taken on a death march from Reichenbach toward Czechoslovakia. Tired, weak, hungry and frail, they were forced to walk for days through the mountains of Czechoslovakia in the bitter cold of winter. They were not dressed for it and without sufficient fat on their bodies to keep them warm and food to give them energy, it took all their strength and inner fortitude to keep moving and not die of the cold and starvation.

After hours of walking, without warning, Ro suddenly threw herself to the ground and said over and over, *"I don't want to live anymore. I don't want to live anymore. Please God take me."* Sonja watched as Ro's eyes rolled into the back of her head just before passing out and collapsing hard to the ground. Sonja, in a panic, took Ro into her arms and slapped her in the face side to side to wake her up telling her over and over with fierce determination, *"You have to live. You have to live. I want you to be alive. We will come out of this. We will survive. We will get out."* My mother told me how clearly she remembers the tears dripping down her cheeks as she couldn't bear the thought of losing her beloved sister, Ro. She knew that if the Nazis saw Ro on the ground, they would likely shoot her dead as she had already seen them do to so many others. Without wasting a precious moment, Sonja picked Ro up onto her back and carried her over her shoulders the rest of the way.

I remember my mother telling me how difficult and excruciatingly painful it was to carry Ro on her back, but she would not let her sister down, literally or figuratively. The roles were now reversed. For all this time that Ro had been like a mother protecting her little sisters, Sonja was now taking care of Ro. When we talked about this brave act of courage and determination, she said that she has no idea where she got the physical strength from. She said to me, *"By this time we were all just skin and bones. We were like walking skeletons so I don't know how I did it."* I believe it was her strength of spirit, sheer stubbornness and fierce determination that made up for any lack of muscle and physical strength. What courage to do what she did. She didn't just save one life by saving Ro; she literally saved all the generations that have since followed, including her three wonderful children, grandchildren and so on. It was *meant to be* that Sonja would save her sister's life in such unlikely and dire of circumstances.

Thankfully, it was soon after the death march that the war finally came to an end. Sonja was not sure how much longer they could survive and keep beating the odds. In May 1945, Sonja and her sisters were liberated by the Swedish Red Cross. Sonja would always be grateful to the Swedish people for saving her life.

Imagine that in 1940, the population of The Netherlands was nearly 9,000,000. Approximately 140,000 of these were Jews; 107,000 Jews were deported to German concentration and extermination camps. Only about 5,500 of them survived the camps. This means that 95% of Jews in The Netherlands who were sent to the camps were killed. [23] Thankfully my mother and her sisters were part of the very small 5% who managed to survive.

After their liberation from the camps by the Swedish Red Cross, my mother and her sisters were taken to Sweden via Denmark. Upon arrival, they received clothing, food, and medical attention and were then sent to recuperate in different locations. I remember meeting an older Swedish gentleman at a party a few years back and told him about my mother's positive experience in Sweden and of the Swedish people. He told me how he remembers as a young child seeing the busloads of ex-prisoners looking like skin and bones, and how he and his people felt such great sympathy for them. He had tears in his eyes. I was so touched by his sharing of this powerful memory from his youth. It clearly made a deep impression on him.

Similar to what happened to John when an abundance of food had suddenly become available, Sonja watched others stuff themselves. Some of those who overindulged for immediate gratification, without thinking of the consequences, ended up dying from overeating as their frail and malnourished bodies could not handle the sudden large food intake. Sonja was wise enough to pace herself and slowly allow her body to adjust to eating properly again.

It is so sad that these Holocaust victims managed to survive the horrific experiences of their captivity in the concentration camps only to die from overeating. What a shame to have lost these individuals as well as all the generations they could have produced.

The Swedes were unable to pronounce Sonja's given name, Schoontje, and told her, *"From now on we will call you Sonja."* That is how her name got changed. This became her name for the rest of her life. She would always say how she didn't mind it at all as she was never fond of her given name and actually preferred Sonja.

As she recuperated physically, put on some weight and started feeling better mentally and emotionally, Sonja slowly began to sing again. When officials heard her angelic voice, they made arrangements with a local music conservatory to offer her a scholarship. She told them that she was truly honored by the offer, but was still feeling too emotionally vulnerable after all she had been through and did not feel ready to commit to something of this magnitude. She refused the offer and chose instead to go back to The Netherlands where she felt she belonged. This was one of those moments in life where I wonder about what would have happened had she accepted the offer - would my mother have gone on to become a world famous singer? Who knows? She certainly had the talent, personality and charisma for it.

Chapter 10

Return to The Netherlands

After a year recuperating in Sweden, Sonja and her sisters returned to The Netherlands. The only living relative they could find who also managed to survive the war was an uncle who lived in Wierden - a town close to Rijssen where they were born and raised. Finding him was a blessing that was *meant to be* as he was kind enough to take the three girls into his home to live. Had they not found him, they're not sure what their fate would have been.

Upon visiting their house in Rijssen, the girls were horrified when they were met at the front door by strangers who had taken over their family's home. They would later learn that this was not an isolated incident. Jews returning from hiding or from the camps post-war all had their property looted or destroyed. The houses Jews used to live in were now occupied by strangers. The Dutch citizens simply didn't expect any of the Jews to return.[24] *"How could this be?"* my mother wondered. *"What gave these strangers the right to take over our family home and whatever family belongings may have been left behind?"* Imagine my mother standing in the doorway of the home in which she was raised. I wonder if any of her family's furniture, paintings and other belongings were still there in the background just as they were left behind that terrible day they were forced from their home through that same doorway where she was now standing. I'm guessing that there was nothing left that belonged to her family. The people occupying the home exclaimed, *"What do you think you are doing here? You were not supposed to come back. This is our house now."* The new home-owners slammed the door on them.

Sonja was filled with despair. It was all so unjust. After all they suffered, how could this have happened? The lack of humanity, unwarranted sense of entitlement, and total absence of compassion shown by these strangers is astounding to me. How could they slam the door on these young women who had every right to be there?

After a few short months, Ali went back to Sweden where she married and had children of her own. Over time, Ro would marry and raise a family. Sonja found a job in Amsterdam as a nurses' aide in a Jewish nursing home called the Joodse Invalide. It has since been renamed to Beth Shalom. The job came with an apartment in the nursing home where she could live. This was a wonderful blessing surely *meant to be,* as Sonja was thrilled to be able to both live and work at the same address. She was very happy in her work taking care of the elderly. The job was perfectly suited for her as she was a very warm and nurturing soul. My mother always had tremendous compassion for both children and the elderly and was always ready with a helping hand, warm smile and open heart. She had the extra patience and kindness required for this type of work.

One day, after a number of years into the job, Sonja heard about a new female resident who had just been admitted to the nursing home. When introduced, the two ladies recognized each other right away and immediately burst into tears. Sonja could not believe her eyes. The new resident was the mother of the identical twins who she saved from the evils of Dr. Mengele in Auschwitz. They hugged each other tightly and could not believe the incredible fate that brought them back together again so many years following the war. How could this be possible?

What are the chances that these two survivors would reunite? How could one challenge the notion that perhaps this was some sort of divine intervention at play? I get the chills every time I think of this story and how beautiful this moment must have been for the two of them. It was a blessing that was *meant to be*, indeed.

Sonja could hardly wait to ask how the twins were doing. The mother was delighted to tell her that they were healthy, happy and well, thanks to Sonja's act of courage. Sonja went to the Director of the home and told her the story of her relationship with this woman and what had happened in the camp. It only seemed fitting that the Director would assign this new resident to Sonja's care. Sonja took special care of her till the woman took her final breath. Sonja remembers how she regarded it as both a privilege and honor.

With her natural beauty, social grace, sense of humor and warm personality, it was no surprise that many men were attracted to Sonja. She went out on dates with a few of them, but none of them were able to win her over. Inevitably, she would find out that they had lied to her about some aspect of themselves, and she would be left feeling betrayed. Trust became a bigger and bigger issue for Sonja. If she did not feel that she could trust her suitor, she would drop him immediately. I remember her saying to me on many occasions, *"Without trust in a man, you have nothing."*

Although Sonja had yet to find the man of her dreams, she did not sit at home alone twiddling her thumbs. She sought out other ways to keep busy, be social and have fun.

One day, while browsing the local Jewish newspaper, Sonja saw an advertisement seeking a talented singer to join an all ladies Jewish singing quartet. Sonja responded without delay, auditioned and was accepted on the spot. Once they heard her pure, pitch-perfect voice, and the feeling she brought to the music and lyrics, it was obvious that they didn't need to look any further. This, too, was *meant to be*. She became best friends with the other three ladies - Claar, Schel and Ria the pianist. The quartet became an integral part of her life. It was her escape, her medicine, her healing, her solace and greatest joy. She also joined a mixed choir under the direction of the renowned conductor Hans Krieg. Although her day job was rewarding on many levels, her singing was what fed her soul in ways she could barely find words for. As we have seen, her singing continued to follow her through her entire life.

Sonja suffered terrible back problems after the war and till the day she passed. I wonder how much of it was from working on the railroads and how much from carrying her sister on her back. She was eventually diagnosed with both osteoarthritis and osteoporosis in her spine. The pain and discomfort were often unbearable. She used to say, *"The back pain I have, I have Hitler to thank for that."* However, I remember her telling me many times, *"No matter how much pain I had, when I got on stage to sing in front of a live audience, that was my best medicine. That was where I felt no pain."*

The quartet sang at the biggest concert hall in all of Amsterdam, singing the rich and soulful melodies so typical of Yiddish and Hebrew songs. She would tell me how you could hear a pin drop, especially with singing Jewish songs with the memory of the war still so fresh in the minds of the Dutch population. Sonja was the main soloist and quickly became accustomed to the many standing ovations she received. She was in her glory.

I have a photo of my mother accepting a medal of honor on behalf of the quartet from the mayor of Amsterdam. It was in recognition for winning a national singing championship. This was an honor of a lifetime for her. In the photo below, you will see how she is the only one looking into the camera and she couldn't have looked more beautiful.

Left to Right: Claar, Sonja, Schel, Ria

Chapter 11

John Meets Sonja

Although Sonja made a successful transition to freedom and was content in her new life, there was still something missing. With time passing quickly, Sonja's longing for a husband and family was becoming stronger and stronger. As she always loved to care for and be around children, it was her dream to have some of her own one day. Her mothering instincts were calling her. She had only the fondest of memories of her own family life growing up in Rijssen and wanted nothing more now than to have a family of her own. She dreamed of creating a warm and cozy home life filled with joy, peace and love.

As the saying goes, *"Ask and ye shall receive."* Do you remember Mrs. Van der Velde? She was the wife of the man who performed the wedding ceremony for my Uncle Paul and his wife back in the Dutch East Indies before the war. I mentioned at the beginning that you would see how she would play an important role in John's life years later.

Here's what happened.

After the war, Mrs. Van der Velde moved back to The Netherlands and somehow reconnected with my father. He does not remember exactly how they found each other. Following my dad's move to Montreal, the two of them continued to keep in touch by correspondence. It's a good thing they did. As fate would have it, Mrs. Van der Velde was now working in the Joodse Invalide and got to know my mother quite well.

Mrs. Van der Velde grew to like Sonja very much. Sonja had shared with her on more than one occasion some of the negative dating experiences she'd had, and how she would really like to meet a good, honest and trustworthy man to share her life with.

Mrs. Van der Velde got an idea. She knew what Sonja was looking for in a man and that John was set up in Canada ready to meet a fine young Jewish woman to share the rest of his life with. She told Sonja how she wanted to introduce the two of them. Having had little luck with men in The Netherlands, Sonja agreed to be introduced. She figured she had nothing to lose and only everything to gain.

Mrs. Van der Velde wrote to John, *'I have a nice girl for you. She works as a nurse's aide in the Jewish old people home here in Amsterdam where I work. I will introduce you to her and the rest is up to you'*.

Sonja and John began to correspond, writing letter after letter to each other. As soon as a letter was received, it would be read and responded to right away. They sent photos back and forth and kept each other's photo by their bedsides.

When Sonja showed the photo of John to Ro, she saw right away the uncanny resemblance that John had to Hans. Hans was Ro's fiancé before the war who she later learned died in Auschwitz. If you remember, Sonja had a crush on Hans and told Ro that if she didn't marry him, she would marry him herself. That's when Ro knew that Sonja would marry John and move to Canada. When Sonja married John, it was in one way like she was marrying Hans because of how much they looked alike. Ro was happy for Sonja, but also sad to know that her sister would be leaving her behind.

The irony is that when John first saw a photo of Sonja, he was struck by the strong resemblance she had to Margo, the beautiful girl he was in love with in Manila right after the war. He knew he would love Sonja the same.

Is it just coincidence that Hans and Margo would look so much like John and Sonja? Isn't it remarkable how they both found their soul mates so many years later who just happened to remind them so much of their loved ones from the past? Naturally they both believed that this, too, must have been *meant to be*. In viewing the photos of each other, there was an instant attraction based on the good feelings for those they cared for so deeply so many years ago. The question still remained, however, whether or not the chemistry would exist between them in person as well.

John was very honest in all his letters. He made no pretenses about who he was as a person and what he had to offer. Sonja was impressed with his honesty and was not concerned that he did not have lots of money. She was happy to know that he was a hard worker, honorable and trustworthy. This meant more to her than anything money could ever buy. She did not worry about money. Although she appreciated good quality clothing, shoes and the necessities of life, my mother was one of the least materialistic and lowest maintenance women I've ever known. The older I get, the more I realize how much I am like her in this regard. I learned from her to care more about the things of true value in life such as health, people and relationships versus fancy clothes, expensive jewelry and other material things.

After only four months of corresponding, John and Sonja decided it was time to meet. John planned to spend his vacation days in The Netherlands with Sonja.

Their anticipation grew as their meeting got closer and closer. They could hardly contain themselves with their mounting impatience and excitement. With each letter they were literally counting down the days. Neither of them had ever experienced such intensity of positive emotions for another person. They were like teenagers in love. The only thing was for them to see if they would feel the same way in person as they did through the letters.

The day finally came. John arrived in The Netherlands and they saw each other for the first time. A photo was taken when they arrived in Sonja's apartment. The photo below is my favorite photo of the two of them.

John & Sonja in Sonja's apartment when they first meet in The Netherlands.

The expression in their faces and look in their eyes as they gaze at one another gives me a feeling of joy that never fades. I remember them telling me how they both knew instantly that there was no turning back. They knew they were *meant to be* together for life, and without hesitation, got married on July 29, 1960, with a civil ceremony in Amsterdam. Now legally husband and wife, it would make it easier and faster for Sonja's immigration to Montreal, Canada.

You might be wondering how I know so much about what was in the actual letters. After my mother passed away on January 14, 2004, I had the painful task of sorting through all her personal belongings. While emptying her dresser, I found to my most wonderful surprise all of my parents' love letters in a bag tucked neatly away in the back of one of the drawers. My mother was not one to hold onto things from the past. She despised clutter, but she was wise enough to save these letters.

I remember opening the bag not realizing at first what was inside. Then I saw the letters with all the stamped envelopes to go with them dating back from March to October of 1960. There are no words to describe how full and elated I felt inside my heart. It was exciting to me beyond belief, yet at the same time, I could not bring myself to read them right away. I read one or two aloud to my dad but could barely finish reading them through the veil of sobbing tears. It got so bad that I couldn't even see the words on the page and was afraid my tears would smudge the ink. In time, I was able to read through them all letter by letter, word by word.

There are 204 pages of letters all hand-written in Dutch. Thank goodness I can read and understand Dutch fluently. It was nine years after my mother's passing before I knew I was ready to read the letters. I finally took the pile in hand and painstakingly read and translated each one into English.

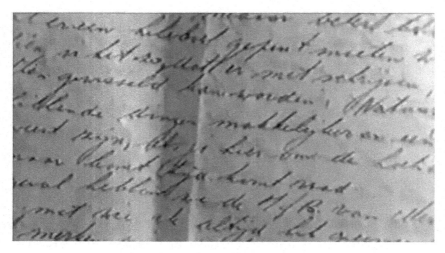

Excerpt from a letter from John to Sonja

I kept a box of tissues by my side. I became obsessed with translating the letters and could hardly do anything else. I could not have been happier when my father gave me his approval and blessing to translate them all into English. I would on occasion sit with my father reading the letters to him in Dutch and he would marvel at them. He would say to me with a sheepish grin, *"Did I write that? I didn't know I was such a romantic."* The letters are truly beautiful. I consider them to be a precious gift providing so much insight into my parents' psyche as two young people falling in love. Not many people get the opportunity to know their parents on such a personal level as what they were like before being brought into their lives.

Here are some excerpts from the letters that struck me. They truly demonstrate the personal values and wisdom my parents both shared.

Sonja:

I'm a very simple girl and what you see is what you get. I give myself as I am. I love a cozy home life. I enjoy singing and love good music and going out from time to time to the theatre or a beautiful opera or concert. I have a wonderful collection of beautiful music. I don't have my parents anymore, but I still have two sisters; one in The Netherlands and a twin sister in Sweden. Too bad that you live all the way in Canada as it would be much easier if you lived in The Netherlands so we could have much more contact with each other.

John:

I am 5' 5" or in Dutch measurement 1 meter 65 cm and weigh approximately 170 pounds. My hair is beginning to turn gray a little on the sides, but that's probably because life has not come to me without hardships.

Sonja:

Yes, life for us was not easy and we have suffered much. I have also been in the camps in Germany and Poland, but that we must try as much as possible to forget even though that is not so easy to do. Life goes on and we must look ahead of us and leave our suffering behind. That's why it's so important to understand each other and to be open and honest with each other.... As far as being religious is concerned, that I am not, however, I do like the traditions and making the house a home and cozy on the special holidays because in my heart I am a Yiddishe girl, after all, if that's how you want to call it... Because what does it mean to be religious? In my belief, you are religious if you go through life honestly and are good for the most people as possible. That is my outlook. We are in the world to help each other. Because many people are religious for appearances, for the outside world, but that I do not like. I really am a believer, though...

Understanding each other is indeed a big word but where there's a will there's a way. In the whole world there are also not two people who are exactly alike and everyone makes mistakes. As soon as you see some sort of faults we should try to express it and talk about it because then you are already on a good path.

John:
You look very sweet from your photo. It is lying now beside me while I write and then it is just like I am talking with you. But it doesn't feel strange for me. It is just as if I have known or seen you before. Crazy, eh? I am still from time to time a romantic. I can't help it.

Tell me something about yourself. What color eyes do you have? Do you like to dance? And which ones? Where did you live in The Netherlands before you came to Amsterdam? What are the things you like to do? You like to go for walks? You ever go to the walking park? I liked to do that when I lived in Amsterdam. I found it to be wonderful. Now dear Sonja, I will end it again and until we write again. Next time a little bit more from here.

Sonja:
I love to dance too, but hardly ever do it as there are so few men of my age, most are much younger and I feel then so unhappy when

I'm at one of those evenings. So then I'd rather not go. Now if you were in Amsterdam, then that would be cozy. How we would talk so much with each other, as a person has and needs to have through this someone that you truly can trust and share your heart with, without anyone else there, and understand each other. Walking I enjoy very much, and I like nature a lot, but can't go sitting as a girl alone in the walking park. I would say, come for vacation to The Netherlands and then we would go together to the park and schmooze.

John:
You mustn't forget, that if you're thinking toward security, then you are mistaken. I do not have a big bank book or relations with such, but am just a an ordinary young man who wants to work hard, and the time in this world is too short in that there's so much yet to see and enjoy.

Sonja:
Have such a feeling that I've seen you years ago. I also have a trusting feeling as I speak with you like this. Would very much like to see you and speak with you as our characters, I believe, can get over many things.

John decides to take his vacation in The Netherlands to spend time with Sonja. They are both counting down the days, but Sonja does not want to let her emotions rule her.

Sonja:
If it will be something between us, we will learn in time. We will learn about each other, and see if we dare together, but will do

nothing in haste, as that is not good. When you are first together everything is beautiful, but we have to both think everything over.

Yeah, those camps did not do us much good. I was in the camps myself also.... I went through a lot, too, and that's why a person can also show more understanding for another. As someone who was not there, they don't know what it is, and that is a good thing too. Singing is for me a very big healing.

John:
Dearest Sonja, don't you find it wonderful that we can understand each other so well? I find that a really good foundation, and if you can simply talk to each other then it is wonderful, that's at least how I'm feeling about it. There is enough sorrow in the world, and if together we can make it easier, why not?

You know that we all strive toward an ideal, but somewhere we must make a compromise. We are all just simple people with faults and defects and will try to get on with each other, that is at least how I find it. Don't forget that we have necessary experiences and especially for you, as you so write, that you work so close to the dead, that life is actually very short and too short to throw away, and on the other side again too beautiful not to make everything of it, as it is the purpose of the universe to make each other happy. Naturally, you don't have to sacrifice yourself, but small and if necessary big sacrifices, if you know that without, you're making the other happy. It is so most often the small things that are important that makes the marriage. It is exactly what you make of it.

John visits Sonja in The Netherlands and they get married. John must go back to Montreal and Sonja must stay behind in The Netherlands to get all her affairs and papers in order to immigrate to Canada. Now that they are married, they can hardly wait to be together again.

Sonja:
Now, we must be strong and wait out time, and that time will truly come, even if it takes for us both still so long. I, too, find it wonderful if I think so intensely about my John, then there goes such a nice feeling through me. John, what more can I write you than that we truly love each other so pure and sincere. I find it so wonderful that you love me so much, but that is from my side just the same, and I long very much for you.

I believe that finding the letters was no simple accident or coincidence. It was truly *meant to be*. I had no idea when I originally found them that I'd be writing this book and sharing their stories. I just knew that it was a gift that I would treasure for the rest of my life. As mentioned, I wasn't able to read them all right away, as it was just too difficult so soon after my mother's passing. However, by the time I was ready to read through them all, I had already decided that their story was one that the world deserves to hear. That was when I made the commitment to share their unforgettable story through this book, my speaking tour and as a film. My hope and wish is that my father will live to see it all. I truly believe in my heart that my mother is also with me throughout this whole process from wherever she may be in this universe or beyond.

In reflecting on my mother's complete trust and faith in my father and their budding love for one another, I have the utmost respect and admiration for my mother's courage. Moving to a new country for a man she fell in love with through correspondence, who she had barely spent time with in person, knowing very little of the country she was about to move to, and not even speaking English, was truly a marvel.

Some people may think she was crazy to do such a thing. They may think about all the risks she was taking and question how she could leave her whole life, family and friends behind in The Netherlands for so much uncertainty. What they don't understand is that my mother was not thinking about what she was leaving behind. She was only thinking about all she had to look forward to, and all she had to gain. She was not afraid of learning English. She was not worried about what if it didn't work out. She just dove right in with both feet, full of enthusiasm, eagerness and excitement. All she could see were possibilities. She would take everything as it comes, one day at a time, just like she had learned to do in the concentration camps, as that was all one could do in those most uncertain circumstances.

On October 23, 1960, Sonja finally arrived in Montreal. John naturally greeted her at the airport with big hugs and kisses. He then took her directly to the home of Rabbi Spiro where she lived for a week prior to the wedding. In accordance with religious Jewish custom, the bride is not allowed to see the groom for seven days prior to the wedding. I can't even imagine how difficult this must have been for my parents, especially my mother. Here she was with strangers in a strange land not speaking the language. Sonja, being the trooper that she always was, simply did her best to adjust, get along and go with the flow. As the Rabbi and his wife were very close friends of John, they were beyond delighted to host Sonja in their home. It must have been so difficult for my father as well. He finally had his beloved Sonja by his side and then he could not see her for a whole week. On the positive side, it just meant that much more when they finally would see each other at the wedding.

John and Sonja had the Jewish wedding ceremony and celebration on an unusually warm, beautiful and sunny day, on October 30, 1960, which they marked as their true wedding anniversary for the next forty-four years. It was a joyous and boisterous celebration. From the 8mm home movie of the wedding, it is easy to see how Sonja was delighted, singing, smiling and nodding the whole time with the utmost of grace.

After the wedding, John and Sonja settled into the one room basement apartment that John found for them while Sonja was still in The Netherlands. John painted the walls and they decorated the apartment together. Sonja unpacked the crates of her belongings that were carefully shipped by boat. She kept her promise from her letters to create a warm, tidy and cozy home atmosphere. This meant the world to her. She had the freedom to finally fulfill this dream and so she did. And she did it very well.

I believe that my mother's need for order and cleanliness was largely her nature, however, I also wonder if it was even more exaggerated because of the filth, chaos and dreadful living conditions she endured during her time in the camps.

Part II

Health Obstacles

Chapter 12

Sonja's Cancer

In January 1983, Sonja's life was turned upside down once again. As she knew from her past, life can change on a dime. That's exactly what happened when her doctor told her three of the scariest words you could ever hear come out of a doctor's mouth – "*You have cancer.*" She was only fifty-six years old. I was seventeen at the time.

The shocking news of my mother's cancer diagnosis did not just turn her world upside down; life as I knew it would also never be the same. I remember feeling very sad and angry. Had she not suffered enough in her life? I just couldn't understand it. How could this, too, be *meant to be*? I was angry with God, as I'm sure you can imagine. I was also very afraid. I remember how terrified I was at the thought of losing her. And what was it like for my father to fear the loss of his soulmate who he had waited for his whole life? I never spoke about this with him. After the initial shock, I realized in time that it was not for me to question or understand why this was happening to my mother and my family. It was just something for me to accept and deal with as best I could. This meant being there for my mother as she had always been there for me. I have to believe that her cancer was *meant to be* regardless of how unfair it seemed.

It all started with my mother having unusual abdominal pain. After some medical investigation, it turned out that she needed to have one of her ovaries removed. It was to be a routine surgery, nothing out of the ordinary. However, during the operation, the surgeon saw to his surprise and dismay that the lining of her abdomen was full of cancerous growths. She was diagnosed with a rare form of cancer called Primary Peritoneal cancer. It was in its advanced stages, yet it never showed up on any x-rays or scans so was completely unexpected. The doctors assured her that the pain in her abdomen was due to her troubled ovary and not the cancer. This led me to believe that if she was destined to have cancer, then it was *meant to be* for her ovary to cause her pain in order for her cancer to be discovered. In looking at it this way, I found something to be grateful for amidst the tragedy which made it a bit easier for me to cope with and accept. I have since learned that if you look hard enough, you can usually find something to be grateful for amidst your hardship, or in times when life just seems so unfair. Having said this, it doesn't take away the pain, but it just makes it a bit easier to endure.

Based on the textbook cases of this rare type of cancer at this advanced stage, and the strongest chemotherapy treatment available at the time, the doctors did not expect my mother to live for more than two years. Of course, her doctors didn't know who they were dealing with.

After all my mother suffered in her life up until this time, I'm sure you'd agree how easy it would have been for her to feel sorry for herself and play the victim. Not my mother. She would have none of that. Instead, when the surgeon told her the frightening news, she looked him straight in the eyes and said to him while pointing to the tattooed number on her arm, *"You see this number on my arm from Auschwitz? Hitler didn't get me, neither will my cancer. I have too much to live for."* This is truly remarkable, wouldn't you agree? She was not about to take her cancer lying down. My mother would fight it with everything she had.

Let's face it, my mother survived so much and had finally come to a place in her life where she was living her dream of having a loving husband, a cozy home life with children of her own to love and nurture, that she was not about to give up now, just like that. She survived the gas chambers on three separate occasions. She survived starvation and the terrible living conditions of the concentration camps. She survived the loss of her family, her home, all her material belongings and all the innocence of her youth. She survived the hard slave labor and brutal treatment at the hands of her evil captors. If she could conquer all of that, she knew she could beat her cancer, too.

With the same courage, resilience and tenacity that got her through her past pain, loss and adversities, my mother defied all of her doctors' expectations. Instead of the two years they hoped and anticipated she would live, she lived for another twenty-one years. During those years her cancer came back five times. Each time she bounced right back up and fought it again. She never let it knock her down. In all those years, if you ever asked her how she was doing, she would tell you in her little Dutch accent, *"Me, I am like the Energizer® batteries, I just keep going and going."* My parents used to keep this little toy Energizer Bunny® on the wall unit in our living room to represent my mother's 'keep going' attitude.

I had no idea at the time how her words, *"just keep going and going,"* would later influence my life in facing my own cancer.

Chapter 13

My Turn at Cancer

In January 1995, my life was turned upside down because of cancer once again, only this time I was the one on the receiving end of the diagnosis. I was only twenty-nine years old when the doctor told me those same three scary words that were told to my mother - *"You have cancer."*

About six weeks prior, I had woken up at 3:00am with a very swollen neck. It was also extremely painful. I thought I might have been having an allergic reaction to something I'd eaten that night. I wish I'd been so lucky. After monitoring it for a few weeks, and my doctor ruling out an allergic reaction, a virus and mononucleosis, he decided to send me for an ultrasound. The results of the ultrasound showed a possibility of Hodgkin's Lymphoma (cancer of the lymph nodes), which a biopsy surgery later confirmed.

From the time of the ultrasound to the time of the diagnosis I felt like my life stood still. Knowing that I 'might' have cancer was devastating, but at least there was still some hope that I 'might not' have it. I did my best to cling on to the hope that it just couldn't be true – that I did not have cancer. When the biopsy results came back and my hopes and optimism were replaced by the crushing reality of my confirmed cancer diagnosis, I was instantly filled with panic. Tremendous fear, stress and worry ensued as I began to wonder things like, *'What's going to happen to me? Am I going to die? How am I going to tell my parents, especially my mother who is going through cancer treatments of her own at the same time? What's going to happen to my job and ability to earn an income? How will we make ends meet?'*

Telling my mother was one of the hardest things I've ever had to do. I knew it would break her heart. At first I didn't even want to tell her so that I could protect her from the heartache I knew it would cause. However, as she was going through her own cancer treatments at the same time and I, therefore, wanted to spend time with her, I knew I would have to tell her. After all, just from my appearance looking like a cancer patient, it would not have been something I could easily hide. Of all people, she would certainly know better.

I tried so hard to be positive and matter of fact when I finally told her the frightening news, but when she broke down into tears, I could not hold back crying my own tears any longer. I remember her crying out between sobs, *"Oh God, why my young daughter? Give it to me, I can take it, but not my little girl. Why? Why?"* It was not easy for either of us. I was so wrapped up in my own despair that it was only much later that I really stopped to think of how hard it must have been on my dad as well to have both his wife and daughter, two of the people he cared for most in the world, fighting cancer at the same time. The fear of loss for him must have been unbearable.

Little did I know upon my diagnosis of the many discoveries that I would come to make during the next nine months of chemotherapy about myself, life and the positive influence of my parents. I was able to draw tremendous strength from reflecting on how they survived captivity, rebuilt their lives, fell in love and got married, raised a family and conquered major health issues with endless courage and faith. The strength and positivity I inherited from their experiences helped me beat my cancer and successfully conquer many other life obstacles thereafter. I discovered through my cancer journey that I could truly embody my parents' never give up attitude by also adopting my mother's mantra – *"I just keep going and going."*

Discovering the Power of Choice

From the moment of my cancer diagnosis, I was catapulted into a whole new world and language. Everything in my life suddenly revolved around cancer treatments, hospital visits, taking drugs for this and that and managing the multitude of physical side effects such as losing my hair, painful mouth sores, and terrible back spasms, just to name a few. I remember the incredible fatigue which I wasn't used to as a person of high-energy. I had seen my mother go through all of this, and now I felt like I was sadly following in her footsteps.

I hated the process of losing my hair. It made me feel so powerless. With a sinking feeling in my stomach, I would watch as my hair filled the shower drain and wake up to a pillow full of hair. Then one day, it occurred to me how powerless my mother must have felt in all the times she lost her hair: as a child when her mother shaved her head to rid her of lice; when the Nazis shaved her head and she watched her hair fall to the floor; and then again to lose her hair to cancer not just once, but multiple times. Not once did she have a say in the matter. I remember when she was bald during cancer treatments, how she would say, *"It's only hair. I've already lost my hair so many times, so what. It will grow back."* She didn't let it bother her in the least. She just took it in stride. She'd been there before and had no problem walking around the house with her bald head fully exposed. She wore a wig to go out in public, but when her hair started growing back, she put the wig away as quickly as possible. This was how my mother chose to deal with it. She could have easily felt sorry for herself. She could have easily chosen to isolate herself from others and hide herself ashamed of her appearance. That's when I realized that her positive attitude was all about choice. In that moment, I asked myself the question that turned everything right side up again, a question that gave me back my life on my terms and helped me understand how much I could learn from my parents. The moment I asked myself this one life-altering question, I made one of the most important discoveries that helped me beat my cancer and overcome many other adversities in my life. The question was this - *"Do I really want to go through the next nine months of chemotherapy and all its ugly side effects letting my negative emotions of fear, worry and feeling sorry for myself rob me of the positive energy I needed to fight my fight and beat my cancer?"* And that was it.

What I discovered with that one simple question was revolutionary. I discovered that I have an incredible super human power. It was the same super human power that enabled my parents to keep going despite all their pain, loss, and uncertainty of not knowing from one day to the next if they would live to see another day. It was the same power my mother used to help her beat her cancer. I learned that I can be my very own super hero because I now know that I, too, have this super human power. What's amazing is that I've had it all along, I just didn't realize it.

By asking myself this question, I discovered that I had the power to answer it with a simple *Yes* or *No*. This meant that I actually had a choice. The answer was easy - *"NO, I do not want to allow the negative emotions of fear, worry and feeling sorry for myself to continue robbing me of the positive energy I needed to fight my fight and beat my cancer."* With this answer, there was no more room for denial, fear, guilt or shame. I used the Power of Choice to go from fear to fight, worrier to warrior, and victim to victory.

I then looked at myself in the mirror with only a few clumps of thinning hair still left on my head and thought about my mother's courageous attitude. In that exact moment, I decided to exercise my Power of Choice by shaving whatever hair still remained. I was going to end up bald anyways, so I just ended the slow and painful process of waiting for it to all fall out on its own. It was my way of having some say in the matter, which my mother didn't always have. The second I made the decision to do it, I did not waste another second. I put the shaver to my head and did not stop till every last hair was gone. It felt incredibly liberating to have some sense of control with my clean shaven head.

After losing my hair to cancer, I decided that I would never complain about a bad hair day again. The truth of the matter was that any hair day would thereafter be a good hair day for me. It made me realize how stressed I used to get worrying so much about striving to look perfect all the time. Now I just don't care anymore. Sure, I still strive to look my best, but if my hair doesn't turn out perfectly, I find out that my makeup got smudged, I have some food in my teeth, or my purse doesn't perfectly match my shoes, so what. All the things that I used to stress over and worry about all of a sudden seemed so trivial and meaningless. I also learned through the process of losing my hair that even when you feel you don't have a say in what is happening in your life, maybe there are positive things you can do to regain a sense of control and self-empowerment. Taking matters into my own hands by shaving my head made me feel like I was back in the driver's seat, and as insignificant as it may sound, it just made me feel stronger and more in control over a situation that I really had very little control over. The only thing I could control was my attitude and choices. I discovered that even my attitude was ultimately my choice, just as it was for my parents.

It reminded me of how my father did whatever he could to take back some control over his dire circumstances during his captivity. Everything he did to empower himself stemmed from a desire to avoid sickness and keep positive. I think about how he painstakingly opened up that can of prunes with the nail he found on the floor to relieve his constipation and restore his health. I remember how he ripped holes in the cement bags and put them over his clothes to keep warm, and fooled the inspector with the fake welding job just so he could get the welding outfit to keep out the cold. I marvel at how he volunteered to work in the coal mines just so he could improve his personal hygiene with a daily shower instead of one every ten days. These were not things that just happened from him sitting and doing nothing. He exercised his Power of Choice to make these things happen. He recognized opportunities and then made the conscious choice to act on them.

The oncologist mentioned that I might experience mouth sores. Well, have you ever had a little canker sore on your gums or inside of your cheek? It can hurt quite badly, right? Imagine the whole insides of your cheeks covered in canker sores. That is what happened to me as one of the many miserable side effects of the chemotherapy treatments. I remember filling my mouth with ice cubes for relief. It was so very painful. Then there was the severe constipation and the terrible muscle spasms in my back. Oh yes, me and my Demerol pills became very good friends. I'm not normally one for taking pills and medications, but I had no problem taking my Demerol for relief in this case. I truly believe that drugs have their time and place.

I had never before suffered such ongoing and extensive physical pain and discomfort as I did with my cancer treatments. The only thing that was more painful was the bone marrow test I underwent prior to my first treatment. I remember the doctor saying to me, *"I'm going to insert a needle into your buttock to freeze the skin, however, I am unable to freeze the bone. When the needle hits your bone, it will cause some pain."* He failed to mention that the pain would be excruciating for a full five minutes. I remember the nurse holding me down on the table. She kept reassuring me that it would soon be over, but the clock on the wall seemed to be in slow motion. Those were the longest five minutes of my life.

All of this physical pain and discomfort was very foreign to me. I just wanted to curl up into a ball and cry. But, then I thought about the pain and discomfort my parents endured during the war, and how they did not have the drugs, healthy foods, water and comforts of a warm and cozy bed for relief. It made me realize that although I was suffering physical pain, it was nothing compared to what my parents suffered in the camps. I made the conscious choice to turn my thinking around and snap out of my pity-party. I stopped and thought about how blessed I was to be living in Canada, a country with such amazing hospitals, doctors and socialized medical system where all my medical care was paid for. I felt privileged to have access to a fantastic doctor and wonderful oncologist who may not have had the warmest bedside manner, but in his own way

December 1995. Sonja and Roslyn shortly after finishing chemo treatments. Notice number tattoo from Auschwitz on Sonja's left arm.

always made sure I had exactly what was needed from my cancer treatments. I was also blessed to have a job that included a medical benefit plan so that my wig and all my drugs were paid for. I had just started that job six months prior to my diagnosis. Getting that job was absolutely *meant to be* because it allowed me to work from a home-based office. This was truly a blessing as I could work from home and make my own hours. This meant that when I wasn't feeling well, I could just go to bed and rest. As long as I met my quotas and could perform all my job duties, I was able to maintain my full-time job and salary.

How I got the job was truly a miracle and nothing short of *meant to be*. I believe that I was meant to get this job exactly when I did in order to ease my cancer experience. I had just quit a 9 to 5 office job at an advertising agency where I was so unhappy that it was causing me a great deal of stress. Out of desperation and in need of a paycheck, I took a job as a salesperson in a car dealership. Yes, what I'm telling you is that I actually sold cars. It had a guaranteed monthly income and that was all I cared about. I was the very first female car salesperson at this dealership back in 1994. I knew it would be just temporary until I found a job that was better suited for me. I was certainly not able to make sales in the way that they trained me as I am not a pushy person and could not follow their script. So, I found my own way of making sales by treating people the way that I would want to be treated.

One day, a lady named Mary bought a car from me and told me how happy she was to be dealing with a kind woman as opposed to the pushy man who tried selling her a car at the same dealership a week prior. She was so impressed with how I sold her the car that she asked me the following, *"Is this your career choice? If not, I know of a job that would be perfect for you, and I believe that women need to stick together and help other women."* I told her that selling cars was definitely not my career choice and I would love to hear about this job she was referring to. She told me how I'd be working for a book publisher based in New York selling books to wholesalers across Eastern Canada, but that I'd be able to work from a home-based office and only have to report to my boss once a week. I'd be given a company car and get to travel. Are you kidding me? This sounded like a dream come true. I loved the idea of autonomy, working from home and only speaking to my boss once a week. I thought it would be exciting to work for a book publisher never knowing at the time that I would one day be a published author myself. This random stranger who I sold a car to then proceeded to write a letter of recommendation as if she'd known me my whole life, and I ended up getting the job. As far as I'm concerned, I was meant to quit my job at the ad agency and sell cars just so I'd meet this wonderful woman who helped me get this dream job. Who knew at the time how this job would be the best case scenario for me while undergoing cancer treatments? I am forever grateful for how all those circumstances fell into place. If it was *meant to be* for me to have cancer, then I am at least grateful for having had the type of job that enabled me to still maintain a full income. If I didn't have the courage to quit my job at the ad agency exactly when I did, and instead chose to stay there out of fear of change and the unknown, then I would have had to go on disability and suffered a loss of income. This would have just created more unhealthy stress that I certainly did not need at the time. Unhealthy stress is poison at the best of times, but especially when fighting cancer as it can weaken your immune system and interfere with your healing process.

As I endured increasing levels of physical pain and suffering that I had never experienced before, I kept thinking about my parents and all the hardships they experienced in the camps. It kept reminding me of how blessed I was to have all the luxuries of plentiful food, medical care, freedom and comforts of home that they never had. With all this in mind, it always served to put a quick stop to any moments of feeling sorry for myself. With this positive attitude, I considered myself lucky. It just strengthened my resolve and confidence that I would get through this and that I just had to ride it out like they did. I exercised my Power of Choice to simply take things one day at a time, just like my parents did during their time of captivity and in facing their post-war health setbacks.

When I think about how my parents were deprived of their own mothers and fathers at such a young age, especially my mother who literally had her parents torn away from her before her eyes, I find it hard not to cry. It is something that deeply saddens me. As a result, I always felt a tremendous closeness to my parents and desire to fill this void for them. I truly believed that it was my responsibility to make up for all of the loss, pain and suffering they endured. In looking back, I can see now what a tremendous burden this was for me to carry on my shoulders from such a young age. I never felt pressure from my parents in any way. It was all self-imposed. I suspect that I am not the only Second Generation child to feel this way. This need to be perfect in their eyes, to gain their constant approval, and have them be proud of me helped me in some ways, as it motivated me to do well in school and stay out of any real trouble in my teen years. However, as I grew up I didn't know how to be any other way, which impacted all of my relationships. I wanted to be seen as perfect and always wanted to please others with a constant need for approval and to be admired. I believe now that this proved to be in some ways detrimental to my physical, mental, emotional and spiritual health and well-being. As for my cancer journey, all of these beliefs made it very difficult for me to reach out for help and support. Instead, I pretended that all was fine and constantly went at it alone.

Things got so bad with my overly self-reliant attitude, that I actually found myself taking a city bus to the hospital for my chemotherapy appointments. My husband at the time – notice how I say at the time – didn't want to ask for time off from work. Taking a taxi was too expensive. I had no family to turn to and didn't want to ask my friends for fear of being a burden or appearing weak and needy. And so, I opted for public transportation. Could we have afforded for me to take a taxi ride once every three weeks? In reality I'd have to now say yes, of course. I guess I just didn't feel I was worth it at the time, and that I could just as well take a city bus to save a few dollars. How ridiculous. When on chemotherapy, your immune system is drastically compromised making you more susceptible to colds, flus and all kinds of illness and disease. Can you imagine the risks I was taking with all those germs and bacteria floating in the air from people coughing and sneezing?

One day, it came up in conversation with my friend, Liz, that I was taking a city busy to my chemotherapy treatments. She said something along the lines of, *"What are you crazy? You can't be taking the bus. That's ridiculous. I will take you. You just call me on my cell phone when you're finished and I will pick you up and take you back home."* And of course, my automatic knee jerk reaction was to say what I would always say, *"No, no, that's not necessary. I'm fine."* Are you kidding me? I wasn't fine. I wasn't fine at all. That's when it hit me like a ton of bricks. How could I not have seen this before? I realized that I was always there for my friends when they needed help and support just as my parents were always ready to help and support any of their friends in need. That is what they always taught me to do. As my mother said in her letters to my dad - *"We are in the world to help each other"*. That was a strong belief that they both shared and instilled in me from as long as I can remember. So why would I not allow a friend to help me in my time of need? Here's where another one of those life-changing questions suddenly hit me, *"Was I not worthy of a car ride to and from the hospital from a friend while going through cancer treatments?"* The essence of this question was *"Am I not worthy?"* If I did not accept her kind offer, what would that say about my own self-worth? Of course I was worth it. That's when I exercised my Power of Choice in my best interest and gladly accepted.

This was when I discovered that by accepting and receiving help, I was not seen as weak and needy or as a burden, but rather as human and vulnerable like everyone else in this world. That was a huge awakening for me.

Yes, my parents taught me how to be mighty in the face of adversity. They taught me about perseverance and that I always have the Power of Choice in how I face my hardships. However, in applying these attitudes through my own cancer experience, as we've seen, I also learned that it's not just about keeping a brave face. I learned that it is okay to let your guard down and be vulnerable in circumstances where a helping hand, a positive word, a joyful shared experience, or simply a shoulder to cry on can make a meaningful difference.

What if being strong and mighty also means letting go of fear, shame and guilt and being able to reach out and accept help from others because you are as worthy as anyone else? I think about how my mother leaned on her sisters for support and encouragement, and what that meant for her to keep going during her time in the war. I think of my father leaning on his fellow prisoners to lift him up when he was feeling down, and how the youth group in Manila saved his sanity while so many suffered far greater by isolating themselves. They both chose to surround themselves with the positivity of others for sources of strength and inspiration. So if I'm facing a problem or crisis in my life, I now know that I don't have to tackle it all by myself. I will reach out for help and support as I need or just plain want it. I seek out positive people to surround myself with and avoid isolating myself completely. I now know that by isolating myself and not reaching out for help and support in fear of being a burden, the only person I'm really burdening at the end of the day is myself. I know that I am worth it as I believe you are and we all are.

We may not choose the difficult challenges and painful adversities that come our way, as I feel we cannot choose our fate per se, just like my parents did not choose theirs and I did not choose mine. However, we do have the Power of Choice to either continue pretending like everything is fine when it isn't, or we can be honest and make wiser choices with our best interest in mind for what is within our control. For example, you may not choose to get a heart attack, but to minimize your risk, you have the Power of Choice to quit smoking, eat healthy, manage your weight, get plenty of rest and reduce your stress. If you already live a healthy lifestyle and still have a heart attack, then you can feel confident that you did your part to prevent it and have the Power of Choice in how you deal with it with the most positive attitude possible.

In reflecting on all the obstacles my parents overcame, I discovered that just like my parents, I had the Power of Choice. I thought about all the different choices they made. My mother could have cowered to the evil guard who pointed the gun to her head trying to get her to admit to a crime she didn't commit. She made the choice to stand up to him. She could have minded her own business and taken the easier path of complacency when it came to the safety of the twin girls destined for the evils of Mengele, but she made the choice to risk intervening in order to save their lives. After her negative dating experiences with men in The Netherlands, she could have understandably held a closed mind and hardened heart and thereby decline Mrs. Van der Velde's invitation to correspond with my dad. Instead, she made the choice to take the risk and open herself up to the potential and possibilities of love and romance with a renewed sense of hope and optimism. When my father asked her to marry him and immigrate to Canada, she could have said no out of fear of the unknown of leaving her life behind in The Netherlands to go to Canada with so much uncertainty. Instead, she chose to start a new life and face the unknown head on, taking things one day at a time. When she was diagnosed with cancer, after all she'd been through, it would have been so easy to feel sorry for herself and just give up. Instead, she chose to fight it with all her might. These were all examples of her exercising her Power of Choice.

Had my mother not made those brave and mighty choices, she may not even have survived the camps. Maybe the guard would have killed her had she been too weak to stand up to him or showed her fear. Maybe the twin girls would have been subjected to horrible experiments or killed and she would have lived with guilt and shame the rest of her life for not helping when she wanted to and knew she could. Maybe she would have never married and hence missed out on her dream of raising a family had she not chosen to correspond with my dad. If so, I would certainly not be here today. Maybe her cancer would have claimed her life much sooner had she not had such a mighty spirit to fight and strong will to live.

My father also made many choices that helped to save his life. As we've seen, he constantly made choices to do whatever he could to stay warm, avoid sickness and maintain his strength as best he could. He had the Power of Choice whether or not to volunteer to work in the coal mines. Everyone knew how dangerous it was to work in the mines, but he made the choice to disregard the dangers. He trusted that he could survive it and just simply wanted the daily shower that working in the mines would allow him. He was willing to take the risk. His choice to take risks, and ability to see opportunities and act on them were largely what saved his life. This was in addition to the miracles.

Many of the opportunities that presented themselves, in his case, were in fact the miracles. If you think about the pile of cement bags that happened to be there waiting for him, the nail on the floor that happened to be there for him to open the can of prunes, the already welded piece of metal that just happened to be there for him to fool the inspector, the opportunity to work in the coal mines, the newspapers he put in his ears to save his hearing, the advertisement for aircraft mechanics in Montreal just when he needed a job, it just all seems so *meant to be*. My father certainly sees it in no other way. Even if you only believe in random coincidences, you have to admit that so many coincidences one after another to the same person is quite uncanny, wouldn't you agree?

After the war, he made the choice to leave his life behind in The Netherlands and immigrate to Canada. He only had fifty dollars in his pocket, but that didn't stop him. He had the courage and determination to sit in that employment office all day every day for four days till a suitable opportunity presented itself. If he wasn't sitting there at that moment, it's very likely someone else would have gotten the job. Then, of course, there was the next best choice after choosing to work in the coal mines which I believe was asking my mother to marry him. That choice enabled him to finally have what he had dreamed of since a young man - to have a mutually loving and enduring marriage based on love, trust and commitment, and raising a family together as husband and wife.

We all have choices to make in our lives. My mother clearly did not let her fears rule her choices. She may have felt the exact same fears that you or I would have also felt if we were in her shoes in any one of the situations I shared, but she didn't let her fears paralyze her. She did not let her fears stop her from making the true choices she wanted to make and honoring her true self. It would have been so easy to give in to her fears just as it would have been so easy for her to give in to her cancer, but giving in was not her choice. She chose the harder path every time. It served her well and made my mother a stronger person for it every time. I believe that these choices may have helped her in living with cancer as long as she did while defying every doctor's expectations.

Look at how many other lives my mother's choices impacted. She saved her sister's life when her sister was ready to give up and die. By saving her sister's life, she made possible all the generations to follow. She saved the twins' lives, which created the opportunity for many more generations. She gave her heart to my dad and together they brought me and my brother into the world. It's important to recognize that when you admit to your fears and choose to rise above them, take those risks and push yourself outside of your comfort zone for a better life, then it's not only you and your life that are impacted. You are helping to create the possibility of a better life for one or more individuals whose lives will be touched by your better choices as well.

I say 'the possibility' because nothing is guaranteed. Taking risks and going out of your comfort zone to go after what you want in life doesn't necessarily guarantee you're going to get exactly what you want, when you want it, and how you want it. Sometimes things don't turn out exactly as planned. Sometimes they turn out worse and other times even better. For example, my getting cancer at age twenty-nine was not part of my life plan. That was my first hard lesson that life sure doesn't always go as you plan. Like we've seen time and time again, things can change on a dime. I learned that one from my parents as well.

Just look at how their lives changed on a dime with their being taken captive, all they suffered, then my mother coming back to her home in The Netherlands only to find strangers living there and my mother getting cancer. However, from my own and others' experiences, I have seen over and over that more often than not, it's better to make the harder choice, take the risk, try and potentially make a mistake, or even fail, than to not try at all. Sometimes there's wild success and sometimes grave disappointments, but my motto is you just accept whatever comes to pass, learn from it, and move on. You just keep reminding yourself how you got through hardships in the past and then constantly renew that strength within to keep going.

Through the inspiration of my mother's strength and courage, I chose the harder path in fighting my cancer as well. If she could do it, so could I. And if we could do it, then you can, too. It is your choice. I encourage you to consider your choices in whatever challenges you are dealing with in terms of your health or otherwise. If you typically follow the easier path of complacency or least resistance and it has kept you stuck and unhappy, then I encourage you to re-consider your path.

Perhaps you're afraid of the consequences and are stuck on the limiting attitude of, *'What if I fail or make a mistake? What if I get rejected or am not liked or admired?'* or you worry about, *'What if I'm not good enough, or it doesn't turn out the way I want it to?'* Maybe it's time to adopt a new attitude of, *'What if I succeed? What if things work out for the better? What if I'm still accepted and loved? And if things don't work out perfectly, so what?'*

I am not my adversities

In beating my cancer, I learned from my mother to stop identifying myself as a cancer patient. Yes, cancer had claimed her body, but despite all the treatments, hospital visits, side effects and all the suffering, she still did not let it steal her spirit. She inspired me to do the same in beating my cancer. At every family or friends' celebrations, my mother was ready with a smile and a song. As long as she could physically do it, she was up there singing her heart out.

At my first wedding in 1992, my mother was in the middle of cancer treatments for the third time. When it was time for family members to make their speeches, my mother chose to sing instead. She sang a Yiddish lullaby that she used to sing to me when I was a child. It's called *Schlof mein kind.* The richness of the song's beautiful melody combined with her soulful singing left not a dry eye in the house. I was told how all the ladies were in the washroom afterwards fixing their makeup from all the tears shed. She was able to enjoy the moment fully by doing exactly as she would have done regardless of her cancer. She did not think of herself as her cancer just as she did not identify herself as her past suffering and loss as a Holocaust victim. She preferred to see herself as who she was in every moment despite her past or present suffering. I, too, strive toward this attitude no matter what is happening in my life. I do not define myself by my problems, as I am not my problems. When I was struggling with food and weight issues, I had to remind myself that I was not my food and weight issues, as I am not my body. When I had financial distress, I had to remind myself that I was not my debt. When I was grieving the death of my mother, I had to remember that I was not my grief.

Inspired by my mother's attitude of sheer might and positive spirit, I celebrated my thirtieth birthday surrounded by friends in a comedy club laughing at the humor and antics of the comedians. I learned to not let my cancer drag me down or my physical appearance as a cancer patient keep me from going out, being social and enjoying special moments with family and friends. I know of so many cancer patients who can only see themselves in relation to their cancer. They let it drag them down and isolate themselves from family and friends. They don't celebrate their birthdays as they don't want to acknowledge that they're another year older for fear of not knowing how many more birthdays they may celebrate. Are you kidding me? I'm just happy to be alive. I will celebrate and embrace every birthday no matter what age. My parents did the same. They always made a big deal about birthdays because they knew how to appreciate life. None of us know how many more birthdays we'll get to enjoy whether we have cancer, some other life threatening disease, or not. Life is a gift. It is precious. I believe that we must celebrate every moment by just doing what we can to maintain our peace and happiness within and help make a positive difference in the lives of others.

While going through my cancer journey, someone told me about a man who was also twenty-nine and recently diagnosed with the same cancer. He fell into a deep depression. He assumed the worst and decided that this was the end for him. He could not get up off his couch and stopped going to work completely. He shut down and isolated himself from his wife and family and refused to participate in any social events. Ashamed of his appearance as a cancer patient, he didn't want any of his friends to see him without hair and with his loss of weight. He allowed the cancer to not only claim his body but also his spirit.

I offered to talk with him if he wanted support from someone sharing his experience. He wasn't interested. It is not for me to judge, as this was his choice. I later found out that after a few months, his wife had enough and ended up leaving him. My then husband did not support me in the ways I needed and wanted to be supported, but at least he didn't leave me at that time. Maybe he wanted to for all I know, but at least he stuck it out with me. I am grateful to him for that. I felt so sad for this young man. I wonder how he is doing today and if he ever did manage to turn things around for himself. I wonder if he ever beat his cancer and if his wife ever returned to him.

Many people go through life looking backwards in their rearview mirrors that they fail to see the many roads paved with potential and possibility ahead of them. By looking backwards or staying stuck in the moment, they risk crashing. They allow their difficult past or present circumstances to dictate their futures and don't believe that they can possibly change paths. I don't waste time dwelling on looking into my own life's rearview mirror. I know that if I do, then I'd just be missing out on the potential and possibilities of what could be waiting in store for me.

I can only hope that this young man survived his cancer long-term and found a way to see beyond his rearview mirror. My wish for you is that you will consider leaving the past in the past, learn from it and look instead at where you are today and where you want to be in the future. Then it's just a matter of mapping out your journey to get there. As my mother wrote to my father in one of her letters – *'Life goes on and we must look ahead of us and leave our suffering behind.'* It may not be a straight and easy road to get to where you want to go. There may be some unpaved roads or ones that are bumpy and full of potholes. You may even get lost sometimes, but if you want to get to your final destination, I encourage you to believe and trust that you will find your way.

I don't remember ever dwelling on a fear of death while going through my cancer treatments. I still do not fear death. What scares me more than dying is not living life to the fullest while I'm still here. I'm more scared of pain than I am of death, so I work hard to live as healthy and happy a life as possible by embracing the Power of Choice in my attitudes, outlook and actions of the things that are within my control. Beyond that, all I can do is accept my fate and deal with whatever arrives at my life's doorstep in as positive a way as possible. As my dad always says, *"What will be will be."*

Whenever I get stuck in a rut, I think of my mother's courage and determination. I think of how she exercised her Power of Choice in her positive mental attitude that kept her going and going like the batteries. I think of my father's imagination and resourcefulness during the war in choosing to do things that were outside of the box and involved some level of risk.

I do believe that things are *meant to be* and we have the power to accept our fate and not live in denial, but that doesn't mean we have to take our fate lying down. If you are facing health issues, or other personal challenges, I invite you to think of my parents and myself and to find your own fighting spirit within and just keep going and never give up.

Understanding the Power of Appreciation

The problem with the Power of Choice, as I see it, is that we don't always feel like we have a choice, do we? Let's face it, our world is so fast-paced that most of us are too busy running around in total oblivion like chickens with our heads cut off. On constant automatic pilot, trying to keep up with our endless To-Do Lists and problems to solve, we are becoming increasingly neglectful of the things that I believe matter most like our health, relationships, and overall sense of well-being and self-worth.

And yet no matter how hard we work, how much we strive for, how much we have, for many of us it never seems to be enough. So many people just have a hard time being happy with what they have. Why? I believe it's because there's always more, newer, bigger and better to be had. That's just what our society values these days, especially in North America. We forget that we have the power to appreciate what we have, rather than focus on all that is missing. Exercising our Power of Appreciation makes us mightier in facing our problems and living a more joyful life.

I know so many people striving to have a bigger house, a fancier car, and more and more stuff and money. It's all about having more, bigger, better. My question is when is enough enough? And the funny thing is that I know people who have far less than others, yet are much happier and appreciative than those with more, so go figure.

There are people who are very wealthy and all they do is strive to make even more money. If that is what makes them tick and keeps them genuinely happy, then that is great for them. I just know that this mindset is not for me. I watch them continually strive to work harder and harder and put more and more pressure on themselves in order to afford their increasingly lavish lifestyles. I'm not here to pass any judgment. I just personally prefer to live a simpler, less pressured lifestyle that I don't have to work as hard to maintain, which for me means less stress. For me, less stress means greater peace. It's all what one prefers and deems important. After understanding the stress my parents endured and having lost my health to cancer, my goal is to keep life as simple and stress-free as possible.

I remember a friend of mine once asking me what I want more than anything else in life. Her goal was to have more money to buy a bigger home. I had to think about it for a while. I realized that all I really want more than anything else is peace. So I make my decisions in life with that underlying goal in mind. If a choice I'm about to make is going to conflict in any way with my need for peace, then I will reconsider that choice and consider possible alternatives.

I believe I inherited this mindset from my parents. My parents were not materialistic. They were never the kind of people who had to have the biggest and best of everything. They always spent within their means and never felt they had to prove anything to anybody by things such as the brand of clothes they wore or the car they drove. My dad only ever owned one brand new car in his lifetime and he was eighty years old when he purchased it. I also remember them saying things like, *"We are not jealous of others who have more than we have. We are happy with what we have."* This came from a deep appreciation for all they had achieved and acquired since the war.

My parents had shared values when it came to money. They were both savers rather than spenders, and were always very frugal and wise with their money. Saving for their future was important to them, as they never wanted to have financial worries in their old age. After having nothing to their name during the war, and for how hard it was to rebuild their lives, a sense of financial security meant the world to them. I believe that this need for security also stemmed from their need to always be prepared for the unexpected. My father to this day always reminds me of how life can change on a dime, just like it did for him and my mother, so it's important to be prepared.

I do believe that I inherited that mindset. We were always a family of what I call 'just in case' thinking. My mother would say *"Take a sweater with you just in case it should get cold,"* or, *"Make sure you have a little extra money with you just in case you should need it."* To this day I am definitely a 'just in case' girl, always thinking ahead of what could happen and that I should be ready. I don't think there's anything wrong with this mindset for the most part depending how far you take it. Sometimes I need to force myself to lighten up as you can't always predict what 'could' happen. In life, I believe that you need to trust and believe that whatever happens, you'll find a way to deal with it. However, at the same time I simply like to avoid unnecessary grief, discomfort or stress wherever obviously possible. This fits in with my need for peace and simplicity.

I definitely inherited the same values about money from my parents. I, too, have never been overly materialistic, or felt a need to prove anything to anybody. I have never felt a need for a big house or fancy car. I, too, enjoy having wise investments and money in the bank in case something unexpected should happen and I can't make my same level of income. After all, as a cancer survivor, I know first-hand how life can change on a dime.

What I learned from my parents is that being content, having gratitude, and feeling blessed for all the good things in life are other wonderful dimensions of the Power of Choice. I call this the Power of Appreciation. To me, gratitude is grace. With our constant striving for more, bigger and better, many of us have lost our sense of grace. We are too busy focusing on all the things missing from our lives, the things we lack and the things we want, that we forget to look around and appreciate all that we do have. I truly believe that we need to make the conscious choice to appreciate what we have if we want to lighten up, regain balance, and just feel better.

My role model for the true meaning of the Power of Appreciation is my father. After all the pain and suffering he endured, and having witnessed the worst of humanity while listening helplessly to the cries of the comfort girls, and watching his friend be shot in the head, he somehow managed to come away from it all feeling that his life is still blessed. To this day he focuses on his blessings, feeling grateful for every day, seeing the good in people, and appreciative for all the good things in his life. Many people find this hard to believe and can't understand it given the horrors of his past.

Chapter 14

John's Heart Attack

In November 1989, six years after my mother's cancer diagnosis, my father had a massive heart attack. He was only sixty-seven years old. I was twenty-four at the time. I believe that it was after his heart attack and emergency quintuple bypass surgery that his appreciation for life grew even stronger than it was already.

I will never forget how I learned about my father's heart attack and what happened after that. I was working part-time at a video store while going to university and had just arrived for my evening shift. The only other girl working that night said to me upon my arrival, *"Your mother just called and said she will call you back."* My mother never phoned me at work before, so I knew it had to be important. Nothing could have prepared me for what took place next.

My mother called back a few minutes later and told me as calmly as she could, *"Your father had a heart attack and is in the emergency at the Jewish General Hospital."* I remember being in such shock that it took a moment or two for the reality of her words to sink in. Then the tears started streaming down my cheeks. I told my mother that I would be right there and hung up the phone. I explained to my co-worker what was going on, gathered my belongings and started heading toward the door. There was not a single customer in the store. My co-worker saw me in tears heading out and said to me in a very stern voice, *"Where do you think you're going?"* I told her what had happened and that I was leaving for the hospital to be with my dad and mom. You won't believe the words that came out of her mouth next. Without an ounce of compassion, she said to me, *"What do you mean you're leaving? You can't leave. Who's going to take out the garbage?"* Are you kidding me? That was her biggest concern? For this one time she would have to take out the garbage. I will never forget my astonishment at how someone could be so selfish and uncaring, so insensitive and inconsiderate, so cold and lacking in empathy and humanity. I couldn't care less about the garbage or if I got fired for walking out. How sad that someone could be so heartless. Without looking back to even answer her ridiculous question, I just ignored her and headed out the door. The only part of that story that I believe was *meant to be* was that my mother was able to reach me by phone because she knew I would just be arriving at work. This was before cell phones, so at the very least I got the news and could be by my father's side as quickly as possible.

My poor mother told me how she had accidentally ventured into a restricted area where she looked through a tiny door window and saw the doctors and nurses using the paddles on my dad's chest to bring him back to life. She witnessed the whole procedure and thought for sure she had lost him. I can't even imagine the depth of fear and sorrow she must have been feeling. She then saw him come back to life before her eyes. Thank goodness, as she, nor I, was ready to lose him.

By the time I arrived at the hospital, my dad was already in intensive care. I was so happy and relieved to see him alive. The first thing he said to me was a comment on the earrings I was wearing which he had bought for me on his recent trip to Indonesia as a gift. The earrings, made from peacock feathers, are truly beautiful. I have always treasured those earrings since then. When I look back, I can't help but marvel that this man had just undergone a massive heart attack, and it was me wearing the special earrings that made him smile and bring him a moment of joy.

The miracle in this story so *meant to be* was that he had just arrived back from a trip to Indonesia one week prior to the heart attack. This was a trip he took by himself to look after some matters regarding his mother's grave. If he had the heart attack a week earlier, it would have happened while still in Indonesia. Based on the more primitive medical facilities in the remote areas where he was traveling, he is certain that he would not have survived. We were all so grateful for this stroke of luck, coincidence or whatever you want to call it that we choose to believe was simply *meant to be*.

He ended up having quintuple bypass surgery. I had never heard of quintuple before. The highest I'd ever heard of was quadruple. He got through the surgery and then it was time to come home, heal and resume his normal life.

I will never forget when my dad arrived home. It was the first time I can remember seeing my father cry. He walked through the doorway and took my mother into his arms and just held her for the longest time. He was so grateful to be alive.

Just as he thanked God when 1) he got out of the outhouse to the bomb shelter in the nick of time, 2) the large metal plate that came crashing down on the straw-filled toe of his shoe and saved his foot which if it had fallen a few inches the other way would have landed on his head and killed him and 3) he was underground in the coal mines when the bomb was dropped on Nagasaki, he was now thanking God once again to have had his heart attack in Canada and not Indonesia.

If he would have had it there, how would we have known what was happening? Did he have our telephone number in his wallet as an emergency contact? We would have been so panicked and helpless unable to go to him, not knowing where he was. It would have been an even worse tragedy than it already was. If it was *meant to be* that he should have a heart attack, then at least it happened in a place and at a time where his chances for survival were much greater and we could be by his side.

My father had worked so hard to get to a place in his life where he was finally retired, living in a home he proudly owned with a wife and kids who loved him. He was truly happy. He would not allow the heart attack to set him back. He was just more grateful than ever, especially now that his life had almost been taken away from him and come to an end.

Chapter 15

Appreciating our True Riches

As I write this book, my father at age ninety-three wakes up every morning grateful for another day. We speak every morning. I'll say to him in Dutch, *"Good morning, Papa. How are things going with you?"* And he'll typically reply with something like, *"The sun is shining,"* *"I just had a delicious breakfast,"* or, *"I feel better when I speak to you."* Rain or shine, he always starts with something positive to say. His whole optimistic attitude and demeanor stems from a place of deep appreciation and gratitude. He not only feels appreciative for everything he has, he is also the kind of person who expresses his gratitude toward others. He will always say to me, *'Thank you so much for the phone call,"* or, *"Thank you so much for the visit,"* or, *"Thank you so much for all your help."*

As I often travel for my work, it is sometimes very difficult for me to be away from my father. I've had to work through my own feelings of guilt for not being close by all of the time. When I am in the same city as him, I make a point of spending quality time with him almost daily. I'm grateful that even at ninety-three he is very adept at the computer and we are able to speak to each other and see one another in real time on video with Skype.

We speak to each other on the phone multiple times a day. I know some people may find it excessive, but it's just what we do and it works for us. Not being close by, I like to know throughout the day that he is okay, and of course it means the world to him for us to have that constant connection, especially when I can't see him in person every day. I've read about children of Holocaust survivors and how this constant need for connection is not uncommon in this unique group of people. I'm certainly one of the statistics.

Many of my friends marvel at the special relationship I have with my dad as they never had that kind of relationship with their fathers. For me it is normal, but I know better than to take it for granted. I understand my dad's appreciation not just for life, but all the little moments that make up one's life. After all isn't life just a series of moments?

When it comes to appreciation, one thing that was always held sacred in my house growing up was an appreciation for food. Very little would ever go to waste. I remember how my mother could perform culinary miracles with just a few leftovers. I'm so grateful to have inherited this skill from her. To this day I have a hard time throwing food in the garbage, or seeing others waste food. You must remember that both my parents knew what it meant to be hungry and deprived of food. Therefore, food was treated with respect. My parents always ensured we ate healthy and that the fridge and cupboards were always well stocked. I remember my mother calling me into the kitchen on many occasions where we'd stand side by side in front of the open fridge and she'd say to me, *"Look what a nice fridge so filled with food. We are rich, sweetheart."* As an adult I still sometimes look into my own fridge and pantry and remember her words. I think to myself *'I am rich indeed.'*

I believe that richness comes in many forms and cannot only be measured by financial wealth. Richness is a fridge filled with good food, a family that loves each other and spends time together, a warm and inviting home with all the necessities. Richness is a good night's sleep and waking up in the morning rejuvenated and eager to start a new day. We are rich when we can see, hear, taste and smell. We are rich when our bodies are mobile and healthy, our minds calm and clear and our spirits high. A key to greater happiness is to both recognize and appreciate our true riches.

My dad often still says to this day, *"Everything is meant to be."* He will jokingly look over his shoulder, and as if speaking to someone, he will say, *"I don't know who you are, but thank you just the same."* I love this expression because it implies his belief that someone is listening and watching over him. He just wants to make sure that whoever it is, or they are, knows that he is grateful for all the blessings in his life. He gets a bit frustrated sometimes because his mind is not as sharp as it used to be. He sometimes forgets names and his overall short-term memory is diminishing. This could be related to his Parkinson's disease or maybe just old age, but he takes it in stride and in true John Franken form, he doesn't let it drag him down. *"C'est la vie"*, he will say which is French for *'That's life'*. That is his way of expressing his acceptance. He accepts things that he cannot change, as he doesn't see the use in doing anything else.

I have learned from him to do the same. There are things in life that I cannot change. I cannot change my past. Whatever has happened has already happened and so be it. The only thing I can change about my past is how I perceive it and what I choose to learn from it. For example, I can be bitter about my failed first marriage, or I can let go of the bitterness and just appreciate the fact that if that marriage didn't come to an end, I would not be the person I am today. My path may have been quite different if I was still married to my first husband. I didn't know myself then the way I know myself today. I did not have the same level of self-worth that I have now. I actually must thank him for helping me become the healthier, stronger and happier person I have become. By letting me go, he set me free. I didn't know this at the time when my ego was bruised more than anything else. However, in looking back I can now see how it was all *meant to be*. The negative experiences of my first marriage just fuel the deeper sense of appreciation I have for my husband today.

My parents always had a deep appreciation for things that many of us may take for granted like a fridge full of food, a nice home, and enough money to live a comfortable life with a little extra for a rainy day. I learned from this to also appreciate all that I have. I believe that after going through a crisis situation or painful life setback that completely derails you from your normal course of life, you can gain a deeper sense of gratitude, and reconnect to what is truly important and meaningful. I count my blessings daily and give thanks to whoever it is watching over me for another day of keeping me safe and healthy with a wonderful husband, beautiful home, and all of life's necessities. Anything that I receive above and beyond these things is all icing on the cake.

When I start getting frustrated with something and feeling sorry for myself, I think of my dad and all the blessings in my life. I think of how grateful I am for everything I have and receive regardless of what might be missing. I am thankful for the following in no particular order: my freedom; my physical, mental, emotional, social, financial and spiritual health; my upbringing; the food in my fridge; the roof over my head; the people I love and who love me back; a loving husband; a good education; a rewarding career and so much more.

A few years back, I read a wonderful book called *The Top 5 Regrets of the Dying* wherein the author, Bronnie Ware, interviewed people at their end of life. She asked them what some of their biggest regrets were now that they were about to die. The one that struck me the most was, *"I wish that I had let myself be happier."* I felt so sad for these people when I read this because now they only had such little time left and they were filled with such a significant regret.

My goal is to live my life today and every day so that I do not have that regret at the end of my life. I am giving myself permission to be happy today and every day. After reflecting on my parents' horrific experiences and the adversities I've faced with going through cancer, divorce, job instability, financial distress, a terrible car accident and the death of my mother, my attitude is that I deserve to be happy and am worthy of happiness. I owe it to myself to be happy now, not tomorrow, next month or next year, but right this minute and the next and the next. I no longer allow myself to fall into the trap of what I call the *'I'll be happy when...'* syndrome as so many of us do. I used to think *"I'll be happy when I lose weight and get in shape... I'll be happy when I find my ideal mate... I'll be happy when I have my ideal job... I'll be happy when I have more money... "*, I'm sure you get the point. Have you ever fallen into this trap? Do you suffer from the *'I'll be happy when'* syndrome? Well, the good news is there is a cure. You can exercise your Power of Choice and Power of Appreciation and choose to be happy today. I make the choice to believe that things in life are *meant to be* and to appreciate the power of might and miracles that I feel are made available to us through our will and spirit.

Chapter 16

Power of Perseverance

After fully recovering from his heart attack and quintuple bypass surgery, John now had the time and strength to move forward in his life with a renewed sense of purpose. In 1991, at age sixty-nine, John participated in his first annual protest at the Japanese Embassy in Ottawa, Canada. He and a group of fellow POWs and civilians who were interned by the Japanese signed a petition requesting a formal apology from the Japanese legislature. The apology requested was for Japan's mistreatment of the comfort women and all the other atrocities they inflicted on the POWs and civilians interned during World War II.

Every year for twenty years, John led a demonstration at the Japanese Embassy for which he received much media attention. In time, John and one or two of his fellow demonstration leaders would be invited into the embassy for a cup of tea. In 2003, a documentary called *Tea at the Embassy* was broadcast on CBC Television. It tells the story of John and Sonja Franken with a focus on John's quest for an apology from the Japanese Diet for all the evil acts they inflicted on the POWs, comfort girls and other innocent civilians during World War II.

As I write this book, my dad is now ninety-three years old. Although he can no longer physically protest at the Japanese Embassy, he continues to write letters to newspapers, seeks out media interviews, and vows to never give up his fight.

My father's dedication to his cause is another great example of his unwavering perseverance. He is not afraid to express his thoughts and make his voice heard. He has been on television, radio and in print in Canada, The Netherlands, Israel and globally through the power of the Internet. My father is also still committed to raising awareness with younger generations by speaking to school children through Historica Canada's *The Memory Project* about what happened during the war, and what could easily happen again, if we allow it to.

By adopting his (what I call) Power of Perseverance, I, too, am ensuring that my parents' voice is heard through my book, speaking engagements, film and whatever other mediums made available to me to communicate their stories.

If there is something you want to achieve in this life such as a dream, goal or a calling from your soul, then I invite you, too, to adopt my father's Power of Perseverance. I know so many people full of potential and talent who have so much to offer the world, but at the first obstacle, they give up on their goals and dreams and throw in the towel. Whatever your goal may be, whether to lose weight, quit smoking, start a business, write a book, travel the world, volunteer for a cause, or other, I encourage you to not give up. I invite you to persevere and continue to do your best, as you cannot do more than your best. Yes, there will be obstacles, and nobody said that following your path, achieving your goal, or living your dream is going to be easy; it takes work. But remember, an easy life is not necessarily a satisfying life. There are many people who seem to have it easy, but are not necessarily happy. Writing this book was not an easy task for me. It took a lot of time, thought, commitment, motivation, perseverance and many sacrifices of other things I could have been doing with my time and energy. The sense of passion and purpose, however, has far outweighed all the challenges that have been put onto my path in turning this book into reality. I have spent many nights lying in bed awake as ideas have come to me of something else I needed to share and include in the book. It was all worth every moment of lost sleep even if it resulted in my being a bit tired the next morning. As soon as I'd get back to my computer and start writing again, I would get a renewed sense of energy and feel as though I'd slept the whole night through.

What I am most grateful to my parents for are the many wonderful gifts I inherited, including the Power of Choice, Power of Reaching Out, Power of Appreciation and Power of Perseverance that we have seen are the best inheritances I could ever receive from my parents and better than anything money can buy. I am forever indebted to them for all they have taught me. It is by applying these teachings in my own life that led to my beating cancer and living my life with courage and positivity.

Chapter 17

My Mother's Death

In January 2004, I was scheduled to travel with my husband to Las Vegas for a conference. The week prior to my trip, I called home and my dad told me that my mother had gone into the hospital. He said that everything was fine and for me not to worry. After all, my mother had been in and out of the hospital many times in the year prior, so this could have been just another one of those times. Something inside me, that little voice that usually knows best, compelled me to call my mother's doctor directly. I'm glad I did. The doctor told me that my mother's condition had turned for the worse and that this was it, she was not coming home again.

I don't know if my father knew and didn't want to tell me, or if he was just in denial and didn't want to believe it. All I knew is that I would not be taking a plane to Las Vegas that week as planned. I would be driving to Montreal to be with my mother instead. From out of nowhere I got this idea to bring my flute, which I had not played in years. As my mother always loved listening to me play, I thought it would be a wonderful distraction from reality and provide her some joy and relief.

The stories of what happened in the hospital that week leading up to her final breath are full of miracles. I know I have given you lots of examples of what *bashert* means in terms of the belief that everything is *meant to be*, but from my own personal experience, the following story sealed the deal.

When I arrived at the hospital, my mother was still in a shared room with other patients. I remember how frail she looked and the big smile on her face when I entered the room. It was as if her eyes had lit up as soon as she saw me. She was still able to communicate at this time. I asked her if she'd like for me to play the flute for her. She was delighted.

I played some of the classic Hebrew and Yiddish folk songs I grew up with such as *Dona Dona, Finjan, Bashana Haba'ah, Hava Nagila*, and many more. However, after a short while, I started to run out of musical repertoire. I had a hard time remembering all the songs of my youth that I used to know and be able to play so effortlessly from memory. I remember how just then a woman came and stood in the doorway of the hospital room. She asked if she could please come in to listen to my playing. She announced that she, too, was a Holocaust survivor and it would mean so much for her to hear my playing such joyous and beautiful Jewish melodies. Of course, I welcomed her to join us. She sat on my mother's bedside. As you might guess, I had a hard time fighting back the tears while trying to continue to play.

I was becoming increasingly frustrated as I found myself playing some of the same songs over and over. Just then I had a fleeting conscious thought go through my mind - *'If only I had a book of Yiddish songs.'* What I meant was a book of sheet music for Yiddish songs so that I could read the music and have a greater variety in repertoire. I don't think it would have mattered to my small audience, but it mattered to me. The thought left my mind as quickly as it came. It was a momentary wish.

Within fifteen minutes or so, a nurse entered the room to announce that a private room was now available and an orderly would be arriving shortly to take my mother to her new room.

Being the curious person that I am, I felt compelled to check out the room ahead of time. I wanted to know where it was and what it looked like. The nurse gave me the room number and I made my way there.

The room was completely bare. It was only as I turned to leave the room that I noticed one thing in the room and one thing only. It was a book lying flat on the bookshelf. I can't explain it, but something was drawing me to this book. I walked over to the shelf and picked it up into my hands. The title said in big bold white letters on a black background *The Big Book of Yiddish Songs*. I wish I could find a copy of this book today. I'm getting goose bumps all over again just sharing this with you now. I stood there with my feet frozen to the floor. I could not believe my eyes. I knew in that moment that my thought was heard by God, the universe, the angels, the life force, the Creator, whatever it is you want to call it. How could this possibly be a random coincidence? It's too uncanny. I decided in that moment that this was God's way of letting me know that my mother was being looked after, that everything was exactly how it's supposed to be and that everything will be okay. I felt so comforted. It is difficult to express. I know it sounds like a crazy story, but it is what I lived and experienced. It was a beautiful moment that I will never forget. I felt a divine connection that was inexplicable and undeniable for me.

After my mother was transferred over to the private room, I lay the music book on her legs and proceeded to play songs from the book. My mother enjoyed it immensely. At this stage, she was still able to sing along with a few lines from time to time. It meant everything to me to be able to give her these moments of pleasure leading up to her end of life.

All of a sudden, this young lady burst into the room. She very rudely interrupted my playing by grabbing hold of the music book. She looked at me with accusatory eyes and said in a loud and menacing tone, *"Where did you get this book?"* I told her that I'd found it on the bookshelf. She then went on to say, *"I am the music therapist here. This is my book. What was it doing in this room on the shelf? It's supposed to be in my library down the hall."* I assured her that I meant no harm. She finally softened up and allowed me to continue using her book. I promised to leave it in the room when I was finished with it. Again, I choose to believe that this was divine intervention. Maybe it was a random coincidence that her book should somehow have been left on that shelf, but I choose to believe otherwise.

I remember one day, sharing this whole story of the music book with my husband's friend who is an atheist. He doesn't believe in God or anything spiritual and that everything in life is completely random. He just laughed at me and told me flat out that I was wrong to even think for a moment that this had anything to do with any outside force. He went on to tell me that it was just a weird random event, nothing more and nothing less.

What upset me most about his remark was that he had the audacity to tell me that I was wrong. Who was he to tell me that I was wrong or right? Here's what I told him back. And this is what I would say to anyone who challenges me on my belief that everything is *meant to be.* I said to him, *"Please don't tell me that I am wrong. You can believe whatever you want to believe. I'm not here to judge you or impose my beliefs on you. However, if what I believe to be true for me makes me feel better and helps me cope better with the loss of my mother, then that is all that matters to me. I can't tell you with 100% certainty whether I'm right or wrong. All I can tell you is what I have come to believe to be 100% true and right for me."*

The message here is that people may not always agree with you, understand you or approve of your beliefs. However, if your beliefs are what make it possible for you to live a happy and meaningful life, then who cares what others think? Who are they to judge you? Please give yourself permission to believe in whatever works for you as long as it is in your best interest and you are not hurting anyone, including yourself.

Over the next week, I lived in that room by my mother's side. I didn't want to leave her alone for a second. My father was there, too. We both slept in the room with her. I was so afraid of not being there with her in her final moments that I even had a hard time going to sleep or going to the washroom in fear that I would not be there for her at her end of life. I kept watching her to see if she was still breathing. It was painful for me to look at her at this final stage as she looked so pale, thin and frail. It was the most emotionally draining and physically exhausting week of my life.

It was difficult to fully grasp what was happening as it was all going so fast. I kept wondering, *'What will my world be like without my mother? What will it be like to never hear her beautiful voice again, to listen to her laugh, to hear her sing, to see her smiling eyes, to feel her warm arms around me?'*

It was difficult to sleep. I slept on a fold out mattress on the hospital room floor and my dad slept on a hospital bed that the orderly was kind enough to bring into the room.

The morning after the first night of sleeping in the room, my father commented on how poorly he had slept due to the discomfort of his bed. He had a terrible night's sleep. Please keep in mind that my father was eighty-two years old at the time. Not long after we woke up and my dad told me about his uncomfortable mattress, an orderly came in and asked if he could trade my father's bed for another. He explained that there was a patient down the hall who needed a bed that could go up and recline, and hers was broken. He traded the beds and my dad slept much better after that. Was that a coincidence, too? I think not. We just couldn't believe all that was happening that kept reassuring us both over and over that we were being looked after. Every time we asked for something, it was received.

My mother's condition quickly deteriorated from day to day, and in the final days from hour to hour, and then minute to minute. At one point she was completely unconscious. We had no idea if she could hear us or not. I've since learned that hearing is the last sense to go and in all likelihood my mother was still able to hear everything.

I noticed she had a tape recorder near her bed, so I asked the nurse if they had any cassettes to play. She directed me to where they had a cassette library. I found one that was all waltzes. My mother loved waltz music, so I decided to play it for her. While the music was playing I got the idea to massage her feet. I thought that maybe it would bring her some comfort without knowing if she could even feel it. I figured that it couldn't do any harm. I started massaging her feet and then all of a sudden she started moving her feet back and forth to the music. With great excitement I called my dad over to come have a look. It was as if she was communicating through her feet to say to us, *"Look I'm still here. I'm not gone yet."* We were so delighted. We knew then that she was still able to hear and that she could hear what we were saying.

On January 14, 2004 at 9:25pm, my mother took her last breath. I can't remember how I knew the end was near. Maybe a palliative nurse sensed it and told me. I have no idea. I just know that while she was still breathing just minutes before she passed, I held her close in my arms and through a veil of unrelenting tears, I said to her in Dutch, *"It's okay, mama. It's okay for you to go now. You have nothing to worry about. Everything will be okay. I will take care of Papa. I promise that to you. Thank you so much for being such a loving mother and for all that you did for me. I love you so much and will miss you so much, but you will never be forgotten and will always be with me."*

After her last breath, in desperation and not wanting to let go, I begged her to take one more breath. I said to her in Dutch, *"Please mama, please take one more breath."*

I don't know why I asked this of her, but after she had passed, while still in my embrace, she did indeed take one last gasp of air. I don't remember another time in my life when I felt such loss, grief and sorrow. There are no words to describe the depth of my despair.

Chapter 18

Beyond Miracles

The miracles that happened in the hospital solidified my belief and faith that everything is *meant to be*. However, there were other moments to follow, a few of which I would like to share with you that helped strengthen my belief even deeper. I know my stories seem almost unbelievable, but that is what makes them so noteworthy. You don't have to agree with me or support my beliefs, but I just ask that you keep an open mind enough to enjoy the stories and at least question the possibility.

In June 2004, only five months after my mother's passing, my father and I went to The Netherlands to celebrate his niece's sixty-fifth birthday. It was a big celebration and with my dad getting older, he figured he should make this trip while he still had the energy and mobility to do it. He was delighted when I agreed to accompany him.

Although we were there primarily to visit with his side of the family, we decided to spend time with some of my mother's relatives as well. We were visiting one of my mother's nephews when one of the miracles began. He came into the living room and mentioned receiving an email from a man living in Amsterdam who was responding to my mother's death announcement that my cousin had placed in the Jewish newspaper. The man who sent the email was the son of Ria, the piano player of the quartet my mother belonged to before moving to Canada. He wrote to my cousin that he'd found a series of photos of my mother during her time in the quartet and thought that maybe someone from her family in Canada may wish to have a few of them.

Firstly, what are the chances that we'd be in Amsterdam sitting in my cousin's home when he tells us about this email? If I remember correctly he had received the email months prior but it was only when we were sitting there in his home that he remembered to tell us about it. That in itself was an undeniable coincidence, if nothing else. Had we not been there in person, we may have never known about the email. Or, was it *meant to be*? Let's see what happened next.

We went to this man's tiny apartment in the heart of Amsterdam. He was very gracious with us. Not only did he show us a few of his photographs, but he then presented me with an old-fashioned scrapbook. The pages were filled with photos and type-written sections that tell stories from the quartet's performances, much like a diary. It included dates, locations and what happened at each performance. There were photos upon photos and even copies of the concert programs featuring my mother's name as the soloist. Flipping through the pages, I felt almost hypnotized by the detailed descriptions and photos. I read that after one of their performances, they went out and partied till two o'clock in the morning. I couldn't believe it. I never knew my mother did these things. It was so wonderful to read about the good times she shared with her friends.

I turned the page and came across the photos of her going away party that her group hosted just before her leaving to Canada. It was amazing to see the photos and then later read about the party in her letters to my dad. I could see in the photos some of the gifts she received, including the set of dishes that I still use today. To see them in the photographs and her surrounded by all her friends made me break down into tears. It meant so much to get such an unexpected glimpse into her history and see what was happening behind the scenes while my dad waited eagerly for her in Canada.

The man was so moved when he saw me crying that he said to me, *"My children have no interest in this type of thing. It would do me so good for you to have it."* As if that was not enough, he then went to his shelf and took down a medal of honor and gave it to me. This was the medal featured in the photo on p. 77 being presented to my mother and her quartet by the Mayor of Amsterdam. After seeing this photo my whole life, there I was, by what I consider to be a miracle, holding this important medal in my very own hands. The feeling was almost magical.

While in The Netherlands we also visited with my mother's uncle in Wierden. He must have been in his late eighties at the time. He was a brother of my grandfather. I had heard about this relative my whole life and don't remember meeting him before. He was like a legend to me as I'd always heard from a young child about this legendary uncle in The Netherlands who survived the Holocaust hidden in a chicken coop at the back of a neighbor's farm. He only came out to eat and stretch his legs. He would have been in his early twenties at the time. I can't imagine the stench, fear and isolation. It would be enough to make anyone go mad, but somehow he got through it and survived after living that way for nearly three years. What's funny is that after the war he actually became a butcher. I can't help but see the humor in that although one might have guessed he would have become a vegetarian to honor the chickens who in fact in some ways saved his life.

After spending time with my mother's uncle, he took us to the neighboring village of Rijssen where my mother was born. I had been to The Netherlands numerous times growing up as a child and never did my parents take me there. My mother never wanted to go back as it would be too painful for her. As a result, I never got to see where my mother was born until this particular trip.

As it was only five months since my mother had passed away, and I was still grieving in many ways, this time with my family meant more to me than words can express. I was highly emotional as we walked up and down the cobblestone streets of her home town. It was like going back in time. Many of the homes had plaques on them showing the year in which they were built. Most were built in the 1800's. Then my mother's uncle pointed out the house where my mother grew up. I could hardly believe that I was given this gift to stand in the laneway between the homes where my mother's uncle said he could still remember her playing with her siblings. I stood motionless visualizing my mother as a child, so young, so innocent, and completely unaware of what was soon to come. Her teen years, which should have been some of the most wonderful years of her life, were robbed from her. It was both heartwarming and heartbreaking to stand there and take it all in. Then we walked a bit further and he pointed out the house where my mother was born and spent the first few years of her life. He told us that all the other houses on the street were destroyed by bombs and only my mother's house remained. I couldn't believe it. Was this another miracle, perhaps?

To this day, I truly believe that everything that happened on this trip was *meant to be*. I also believe that my mother was somehow orchestrating it all. I know it may sound a bit much to some of you, but I truly believe that she wanted me to have the scrapbook and medal as keepsakes, and to finally know where she was born and raised. I felt as close to my mother during this trip as when she was alive. I know she is always with me, no matter what.

On September 5, 2004, I got married to my wonderful husband, Elliott Smith. Elliott is a comedy magician by profession and brings a lot of magic and laughter to my life for which I am most grateful. While on our honeymoon in Florida, we went for a day trip to St. Augustine. For fun we did one of the tourist attractions called the Ghost Walk Tour. That's a tour of special sites where a guide tells you the ghost stories of what happened in those places. They told of people seeing apparitions staring back at them in windows, others seeing ghosts walk by, and more. It was all very interesting, entertaining and we didn't think too much of it. It was just for fun.

In the car on the way back to our hotel, I started to think of what it must be like to really think you saw a ghost or some physical sign of someone who had passed. I said to my husband, *"What if I saw some sign of my mother with my own two eyes? I'd probably think that I've lost my mind."* Just then, at that exact moment, I turned my head to look out the passenger side window of the car. We were driving along the I95 and as I gazed out the window thinking about what I had just said out loud, the very next car that drove by us had the word SONJA written on the license plate. I quickly told my husband to turn his head and look and he just caught a glimpse of it as it all happened so fast. How could this be? There is only one car that can possibly have this unique license plate and it just happened to drive past our car at the exact moment that I asked the question about what I'd do if I were to see a sign of my mother. It was all so surreal. Just putting this story in writing is giving me goose bumps all over again. It was an amazing feeling. That is the only physical sign I ever received, but trust me when I say that it was enough.

Remember about the Power of Choice she taught me? Well, I choose to believe that she had orchestrated this event, too, just to let me know that she is always with me.

Years after my mother passed away, my father was doing some research on the Internet about the choir my mother belonged to in The Netherlands after the war. He managed to find information about Hans Krieg, the conductor. He doesn't remember exactly how it all happened, but he somehow got in contact with the daughter of Mr. Krieg. Through long-distance telephone conversations and emails, he learned that she had recordings from her father's choir concerts on old-fashioned reel to reel tape that she transferred to CD. She sent a copy of the CD to my father indicating the songs where you could hear my mother's distinctive voice as the soloist. I remember when listening to the CD for the first time, hearing her beautiful and unmistakable voice so pure and genuine, how I could not stop crying. What an incredible gift to be able to hear how she sang in those special years of her life. What a miracle for my father to connect with this woman who just happened to have made a CD that included my mother's singing. Talk about the power of the Internet. This was truly a gift for us that was *meant to be* and once again, I choose to believe that my mother had a hand in this as well.

Conclusion

As promised, I have shared with you the stories of might, miracles and triumph of the human spirit demonstrated by my parents' ability to survive their captivity, rebuild their lives and conquer their health setbacks later in life. My goal was to show how the powers of the human spirit, choices we make and our sense of self-worth have no boundaries. We've seen that perhaps things happen that we cannot understand or explain, but are somehow *meant to be*. I also described the many ways in which I was able to adopt their never give up and keep going attitudes in beating my cancer and overcoming many other life obstacles. In looking back at their lives and my own personal experiences, I have come to the following conclusions.

In the book, *Man's Search for Meaning*, author Victor Frankel, a Holocaust survivor himself, questioned what it was that enabled some captives to keep fighting for survival, day in and day out, while others gave up. When I first read this, I remembered my mother telling me how when someone in the camps gave up their will to live and lost their fighting spirit within, she could instantly see it in their eyes. She said that the spark of their will would simply disappear. All things equal in terms of food and water, once that spark was gone, they'd typically be dead within days. Seeing others lose their spark helped fuel my mother to keep her own spark alive. So what was it that kept that spark going for both her and my dad?

My mother simply did not want to die. She exercised her Power of Choice and Power of Perseverance to choose fighting for life over surrendering to death. When she was working on the railroads from morning till night, no matter how tired, fed up, weak, hungry or thirsty she was, and no matter the pain in her back, what kept her going was her stubborn mantra - *"Hitler will never get me."* She was not about to make it easy for him. Thankfully, her physical body did not let her down. When you think of the starvation, hard physical labor, and all the other people who died of contagious diseases, you can only imagine how strong my mother must have been to withstand it all. She was strong and perhaps lucky as well. Or, was her will to live so strong that it in and of itself helped to withstand all the sickness and disease? Was it mind over matter? Is that possible? I don't know, but it is something to consider. Or, was it just a lucky miracle that was *meant to be*? I believe it was the powerful combination of might and miracles that together were *meant to be*, each and every one of them. My mother's incredible might was her choice as she could have given up at any time. However, maybe even her might itself was a miracle and *meant to be*.

My mother did not want to die, but at the same time she was not afraid of death. If you'll remember, she was ready to die when the guard held the shotgun to her head. She would die fighting and being true to herself, but she was not prepared to surrender to death out of hopelessness and fear of living another day. My mother would not be defeated by her circumstances.

My parents had a shared vision for their future that was filled with peace, love and happiness. Their dream was to get married and raise a family, so needless to say they both felt they had too much to live for. They exercised the powers of hope and appreciation by thanking God every day that they were still alive as it meant they were one day closer to regaining their freedom and living their dream. It was what my mother said kept her going. She said to Ro, *"I want you to be alive. We will come out of this. We will survive."* It was as if what she was saying to Ro was a non-negotiable truth. But how could she be so sure? She wasn't sure, but she could not allow herself to believe otherwise. Again, for her, it was just how things had to be. To believe otherwise meant a lack of hope. She knew better than to let go of hope. It was all she could hold onto because without hope, what would be the point of fighting?

When Sonja was diagnosed with cancer, she applied the same attitude. She said, *"Hitler didn't get me, neither will my cancer."* Again, it was like a non-negotiable truth. But how could she be so sure? For her it was, once again, just how things had to be. That was her choice. It was her way of clinging onto hope.

What I learned from my parents and my own cancer journey is that if you have no sense of hope for whatever you're trying to achieve, whether it is to ultimately survive or simply to reach a goal, then you won't push yourself to try and may miss the wonderful opportunities for greater success and happiness. Everything just seems too difficult and not worth the risk and effort. If you don't push yourself to take a leap and try, then you don't have to worry about failing. It's that much easier and safer to just stick with the status quo even if you're miserable. However, you can also choose to make hope the non-negotiable choice where surrendering to complacency and defeat are not options you're willing to entertain. I think not only of my parents, but of those poor comfort women. With what they were enduring all day every day with one rape after another, you would think that all hope would be lost and they'd all just want to commit suicide. Yet, so many of them managed to keep hope alive, and although many did die in the camps, there were many survivors, too. With scars that must run so deep, they still managed to rebuild their lives and keep going. Hope opens you up to courage and the possibility for not just surviving, but the potential for thriving in your life. As the saying goes, *"It's better to have tried and failed than to have never have tried at all."*

When my mother sang the prayers over the candles she made in the camps, it was not just about the lighting of the candles. It was about lighting up the hope inside her heart which was then contagious to all those around her. If you'll remember, the others were frightened at first, but then allowed themselves to soak in the tiny rays of hope, joy and reprieve that came with the light of the candles and the sweetness of my mother's voice. If only short-lived, it was proof that hope was something to be found in moments, and those moments were available to those who opened their hearts to it. Even the Nazi guard could not resist enjoying a moment of reprieve from the chaos. That in itself was also a miracle as it could just as easily been a different guard who would not have let my mother get away with it. For my mother, it was *meant to be*.

We've also seen how both my parents simply took life day by day and moment by moment in the camps. They accepted whatever came and just kept doing their best. Every day that they woke up and were still alive was something to be thankful for. They saw each day as a gift and then prayed for another. They did whatever they had to do to continue believing that the war would soon come to an end and they would survive. They were determined to get out alive and rebuild a beautiful life as *"Life is beautiful and there is so much yet to live for,"* as my father expressed so wonderfully in his letters. The past was to be put behind them, and they would focus on making the best of each other's lives today and every day for the rest of their lives.

Unlike my mother, my father did have momentary doubts with regard to his eventual fate. For example, after surviving dysentery and being so thin and weak, he wondered how long his prison time would last and whether he could survive it when his health had deteriorated so badly. It was the first time that he truly doubted whether or not he could survive. He remembers what a low point this was for him. What kept him going was turning to his friends for comfort and support. They would sit together and talk about willpower and trusting in God that he would take care of everything. They talked about their good memories of home, what the future might bring and about their plans for when they would get out of captivity. Turning to his friends for support was uplifting for him, and helped him regain his confidence and belief that he would make it through.

Later in Manila, he turned to the youth group for support. Just by surrounding himself with positive people his own age and enjoying fun activities, he was able to slowly start to feel normal again. If you remember, those who isolated themselves living only inside the confines of their own minds and past memories, rather than expanding their minds with new hopes for the future and taking in new people and new positive experiences, suffered a more difficult transition to freedom.

One of the most important lessons I learned from their experiences and through my cancer journey is that there is great resilience and strength in the ability to reach out for help and support from others. I now know that the fear of being a burden on others just puts a burden on oneself, and that seeking and accepting help from others is a true statement of one's own self-worth. I discovered that I am worth it and my biggest wish is that you will recognize that you are worth it, too.

There is no doubt that my parents' survival was due to more than just the choices they made in their attitude and in doing whatever was necessary to survive. I believe, as we've seen, that their survival was partly their doing in the choices they made and actions they took. However, there were also what some might call incredible strokes of luck, or what I call miracles that were not of their doing. I do believe that they were being looked after by some higher power that seemed to have a greater purpose for them. Consider the miracle of my mother being put into the gas chambers on three separate occasions. Each time there was a malfunction with the gas supply or they had put so many people through already that day that they had simply run out of gas. This would have meant nothing if in between those times she had given up her fighting spirit and surrendered to death. No matter how strong and positive she was, if there was sufficient gas, then she would not have survived. It was her tenacious and unwavering strength of will and the power of inexplicable miracles that worked in harmony to save her life.

The same is true for my father. It was by his own free will to choose to transfer to the coal mines - a choice that saved his life. Some might say that he did not make the choice in that it was made for him by a higher power. However, I believe it was his free will to have committed to that choice. To me the miracle was that he was in fact given this choice in the first place. That miracle was no accident. My father believes firmly that it was another force at work that was not of his own doing. It was just what was *meant to be*.

I've often heard religious people say that we are all simply subjects of God's will. I am not an overly religious person, but I do believe in some sort of higher power that is guiding our lives. I'm calling this power God, but you can call it whatever you like. I believe that we must have faith and trust in something beyond ourselves to do its thing as it knows what is best for us. However, it makes it sound like we have no say in the matter.

What I believe is that we are in fact equal partners, like co-producers of our own life dramas that play out on the big screen we call the universe. It is up to us to do our part so that God can do its part. For example, there is an insightful joke about a man who religiously practices the custom of placing prayer notes into the cracks and crevices of the Western Wall, also known as the Wailing Wall, a Jewish holy site in the Old City of Jerusalem. The earliest recorded occurrence of such a phenomenon dates from the early 18th century and stems from the Jewish tradition that the Divine Presence rests upon the Western Wall.[25] Every day this man would write his only prayer on a slip of paper asking God, *"Please God, let me win the lottery."* After years of keeping up the practice to no avail, one day, he went to his usual place of prayer at the wall and there was a big piece of paper stuck in the crevice where he usually put his prayer. He opened up the paper and in big writing it said, *"This is a message from God. You have to buy a ticket first."* So there you have it. You can't expect God to answer your prayers and perform miracles if you don't do your part as well. Doing your part may be simply asking a question, having a new perspective, making a decision, or taking action toward your desired goal. Maybe it involves taking a risk, going out of your comfort zone, asking for help, or performing an act of kindness to help another person.

When we look at how my parents were able to meet through correspondence, fall in love and rebuild their lives together in such positive and meaningful ways, there are also lessons to be learned. They both had suffered so much to finally live their dreams in freedom and find true and lasting love, that they would not allow cancer, a heart attack or any other challenge to stop them from living life fully. They never allowed themselves to wallow in self-pity or identify themselves according to their experiences. My mother taught me that when she said, *"Cancer may be claiming my body, but I am not my cancer,"* and, *"Hitler didn't get me and neither will my cancer. I have too much to live for."*

My father was always about living for tomorrow by making the best of today. I know of many positive living gurus who talk about the Power of Now and that life is only about living today, being present in this moment, and not dwelling on the past or worrying about tomorrow. Perhaps this is left for interpretation. Many people tend to live their lives in the past. They are stuck like a needle on a broken record reliving their poor upbringing, abuse, a failed marriage or the like. They can't seem to get past their pasts and move on with their lives. My parents were not those people. They had horrific pasts as we've seen, but they did not let their pasts dictate their present or rule their future. They were always looking at where they were now, where they wanted to go and how they were going to get there. They did not live each new day as victims of their past, but rather as heroes of the day and visionaries for their tomorrows. They had strong values, knew what they wanted, accepted each day as it came, and looked toward each new day with a renewed sense of hope, zeal and gratitude. This is what they modelled for me and how I continue to live my life. People ask me if I worry about my cancer coming back. Honestly, I don't. I just focus on living each day to the fullest and following in my parents' wise footsteps.

My way of not worrying about tomorrow is about making the best choices today that are in alignment with what I want for my tomorrows. I see people who live for the moment simply feeding their animal instincts for immediate pleasure and gratification without regard to undesired consequences and their big picture goals for their future. Consequences are future-based, but if we don't think about them before we act in the present moment, we are fooling ourselves to think that we will ever truly have the life we want. For example, if you want to be slimmer and healthier a year from today, then you have to make the best food choices and start getting plenty of exercise and proper rest in the here and now. Your best choices can, therefore, not be driven by the same need for immediate pleasure and gratification that got you into trouble in the first place. This means you have to think about your choices in the present so you get what you want in the future. Does that make sense? I sure hope so. The trick is to not focus on what you're giving up and sacrificing in the moment, but rather focus on the future gain. This is exactly how I won my battles with weight over ten years ago and have managed to keep the weight off. It's all about best, smart and strategic choices today for the desired happiness tomorrow.

Living in the moment for me personally means to have the presence of mind to make the best decisions now that are in alignment with the bigger picture goals for my future. This is what keeps me feeling mighty within. When it comes to money, I ask you to consider when is enough enough? If you're working yourself to the bone, or stressing out because of all your financial debt and obligations, just to have bigger, better and more things, is it really worth it? I have come to learn from my parents and personal experience that when I value people and relationships more than accumulating more and more things, I have so much greater peace which makes me feel lighter and happier inside and out. If your values around money are hindering your health or happiness, then you may want to reconsider those values.

Other lessons I have learned from my parents and my own experiences are to be true to myself and truly respect and value my own self-worth. It's all about learning to express rather than repress our truest emotions, our authentic selves. By leaving my worries behind and letting my fears go, I opened myself up to so much greater peace of mind and might to face my hardships. By embracing my own self-worth and self-respect, I have ventured to higher aspirations than I ever dreamed possible. Just writing this book took a tremendous amount of self-worth and self-respect to believe that others could appreciate and benefit from my parents' story as well as my own. My feeling is that when you act out of sincerity and greater purpose rather than fear, you will accomplish great things of which you can feel proud.

We also saw how life is short and we can't keep putting off happiness until some future date. Things can change on a dime. That is a theme we have seen throughout this book. I encourage you to stop with the *'I'll be happy when'* syndrome. When you hear yourself saying this, whether to yourself or out loud, notice it, think about it, and then stop it. Just do what you need to do to be happy now, which is simply to make the choice to be happy. This means to be grateful for what you have and stop being the victim of something that has already happened. Let it go. It's time to be kinder to yourself, and there's no better time to start than this moment. Give yourself permission to be happy and live today well so you have no regrets at the end of your life. I invite you to give love and find love, accept love and exercise compassion for others. Remember the co-worker at the video store who was more concerned about my having to take out the garbage than rush to my father who just suffered a heart attack? That was a great example of someone who needs to remember how another person might feel as a result of her words or actions before she speaks or acts. I encourage you to also show others appreciation, empathy, understanding and respect in the same manner that you would want to be shown. It is very difficult to take back words once they are spoken, therefore, I encourage you to also think before you speak.

If people around the world could use their conscious might for desired good, believe that miracles are available to us if we also make ourselves available to them, and remember that things are perhaps *meant to be*, then this world could be a better place. I often wonder what would happen if the entire population of the earth had one common enemy. This is something my father proposed to me years ago. He suggested that if the planet earth was being attacked by a common alien enemy from outer space, it is only then that all the peoples of the world would come together as one to save the earth regardless of race, color or religion. If we all had one common enemy, could we instantly stop our hate, end our wars and erase our man-made religious and ideological borders? If the answer is yes, then why can't we do it now? This happened for my dad in prison camp when he sat around with a group of fellow prisoners of all different religions and ideas of God. They all had one common enemy, the Japanese. With this common enemy, they were all the same and did not hate each other for their differences. They all prayed together as they shared a common goal that was simply to survive. We have the Power of Choice so why do so many choose the path of power, greed, hate and evil when they can just as easily choose the path of respect, empathy, compassion and kindness? If this, too, is all *meant to be*, then maybe just maybe it is *meant to be* this way so we can do our part to change it and make the world a better place.

Endnotes

[1] The Vught Transit Camp." *H.E.A.R.T Holocaust Education & Archive Research Team*. H.E.A.R.T Holocaust Education & Archive Research Team, 2007. Web. 22 Dec. 2014. <http://www.Holocaustresearchproject.org/othercamps/vught.html>.

[2] Camp Vught - Kamparchieven." *Kamparchieven.nl*. The Netherlands Institute for War Documentation. Web. 22 Dec. 2014. <http://www.kamparchieven.nl/en/camps-in-the-netherlands/camp-vught>.

[3] Rosenberg, Jennifer. "The Sobibor Death Camp." *About Education*. About.com, 2014. Web. 22 Dec. 2014. <http://history1900s.about.com/od/Holocaust/a/sobibor.htm>.

[4] "Dutch Jews Killed at Mauthausen Concentration Camp." *Scrapbookpages Blog (Further Glory)*. 18 Mar. 2011. Web. 22 Dec. 2014. <https://furtherglory.wordpress.com/2011/03/18/dutch-jews-killed-at-mauthausen-concentration-camp/>.

[5] "Comfort Women." *Wikipedia the Free Encyclopedia*. WIKIPEDIA, 8 Dec. 2014. Web. 22 Dec. 2014. <http://en.wikipedia.org/wiki/Comfort_women>.

[6] Franken, John. "Fukuoka II." *Kumpulana - Dutch-Canadian Survivors of Japanese Prison Camps*. Editor Ria Koster, 2010. Web. 22 Dec. 2014. <http://www.kumpulana.ca/stories/Fukuoka_II.html>.

[7] "Transit Camps in the Netherlands." *Aktion Reinhard Camps*. ARC - Aktion Reinhard Camps, 6 Aug. 2006. Web. 23 Dec. 2014. <http://www.deathcamps.org/reinhard/dutchcamps.html>.

[8] Fin, Olga. "Shabbat Candles in Auschwitz." *Chabad.org*. Chabad.org, a Division of the Chabad-Lubavitch Media Center, 2011. Web. 23 Dec. 2014. <http://www.chabad.org/library/article_cdo/aid/1457723/jewish/Shabbat-Candles-in-Auschwitz.htm>.

[9] Rosenberg, Jennifer. "Auschwitz Concentration and Death Camp." *About Education*. About.com, 2014. Web. 23 Dec. 2014. <http://history1900s.about.com/od/Holocaust/a/auschwitz.htm>.

[10] "Auschwitz Concentration Camp." *Wikipedia the Free Encyclopedia*. WIKIPEDIA, 13 Dec. 2014. Web. 23 Dec. 2014. <http://en.wikipedia.org/wiki/Auschwitz_concentration_camp.>.

[11] Rosenberg, Jennifer. "Auschwitz Concentration and Death Camp." *About Education*. About.com, 2014. Web. 23 Dec. 2014. <http://history1900s.about.com/od/Holocaust/a/auschwitz.htm>.

[12] Rosenberg, Jennifer. "Auschwitz Concentration and Death Camp." *About Education*. About.com, 2014. Web. 23 Dec. 2014. <http://history1900s.about.com/od/Holocaust/a/auschwitz.htm>.

[13] Louis Bülow, Louis. "Josef Mengele, The Angel of Death" Web. 2011-13. <http://www.mengele.dk/>.

[14] Meals in the Concentration Camps." *The Holocaust Explained*. The London Jewish Cultural Centre, 1 Jan. 2011. Web. 3 Dec. 2014. <http://www.theHolocaustexplained.org/ks3/the-final-solution/auschwitz-birkenau/meals/#.VJkdNBsBh>.

[14] Meals in the Concentration Camps." *The Holocaust Explained*. The London Jewish Cultural Centre, 1 Jan. 2011. Web. 3 Dec. 2014. <http://www.theHolocaustexplained.org/ks3/the-final-solution/auschwitz-birkenau/meals/#.VJkdNBsBh>.

[15] "Auschwitz-Birkenau: Living Conditions, Labor & Executions." *Jewish Virtual Library*. American-Israeli Cooperative Enterprise, 1 Jan. 2014. Web. 23 Dec. 2014. <http://www.jewishvirtuallibrary.org/jsource/Holocaust/auconditions.html>.

[16] "Auschwitz-Birkenau: Living Conditions, Labor & Executions." *Jewish Virtual Library*. American-Israeli Cooperative Enterprise, 1 Jan. 2014. Web. 23 Dec. 2014. <http://www.jewishvirtuallibrary.org/jsource/Holocaust/auconditions.html>.

[17] Koker, David, and R. J. Van Pelt. *At the Edge of the Abyss: A Concentration Camp Diary, 1943-1944*. Evanston, Ill.: Northwestern UP, 2012. 343. Print.

[18] Franken, John. "Fukuoka II." *Kumpulana - Dutch-Canadian Survivors of Japanese Prison Camps*. Editor Ria Koster, 2010. Web. 22 Dec. 2014. <http://www.kumpulana.ca/stories/Fukuoka_II.html>.

[19] Franken, John. "Fukuoka II." *Kumpulana - Dutch-Canadian Survivors of Japanese*

[20] Franken, John. "Fukuoka II." *Kumpulana - Dutch-Canadian Survivors of Japanese Prison Camps*. Editor Ria Koster, 2010. Web. 22 Dec. 2014. <http://www.kumpulana.ca/stories/Fukuoka_II.html>.

[21] Franken, John. "Fukuoka II." *Kumpulana - Dutch-Canadian Survivors of Japanese Prison Camps*. Editor Ria Koster, 2010. Web. 22 Dec. 2014. <http://www.kumpulana.ca/stories/Fukuoka_II.html>.

[22] "Burma Railway." *Wikipedia, the Free Encyclopedia*. WIKIPEDIA. Web. 26 Dec. 2014. <http://en.wikipedia.org/wiki/Burma_Railway>.

[23] "Persecution and Deportation of the Jews in the Netherlands 1940-1945." *Dutch Auschwitz Committee*. The Netherlands Auschwitz Committee

Foundation. Web. 23 Dec. 2014. <http://www.auschwitz.nl/en-exposition/introduction.>.

[24] "Rebuilding." *Holocaust and Resistance in World War II Netherlands*. Web. 23 Dec. 2014.
<http://www.hw.com/academics/ushistory/independent/Rebuilding.htm>.

[25] Placing notes in the Western Wall. " *Wikipedia the Free Encyclopedia*. WIKIPEDIA, 23 Oct. 2014. Web. 23 Oct. 2014.
<http://en.wikipedia.org/wiki/Placing_notes_in_the_Western_Wall>

About the Author

Roslyn is a proud young adult cancer survivor who knows the power of emotional resilience in the face of change, challenge and adversity. She was born in Montreal, Canada, to a mother who suffered the concentration camps in Nazi Germany and a father who survived the Nagasaki atomic bomb as a prisoner of war in Japan.

When diagnosed with Hodgkin's Lymphoma at the young of age twenty-nine, Roslyn quickly learned how she inherited her parents' perseverance and positivity as she herself fought back to become a long-term survivor. Then age thirty-nine, at her heaviest weight and concerned for her health, Roslyn decided to fight back once again - only this time to win her battles with food, stress and lifestyle challenges, once and for all!

As an acclaimed author, international speaker and personal development coach, Roslyn now shares her parents' compelling survival stories, insights from her cancer journey and the proven life principles and practical wisdom that have helped thousands of people world-wide lighten up for good to a healthier, happier and more resilient life.

Roslyn has a Master's degree in Applied Human Sciences specialized in Human Systems Intervention from Concordia University in Montreal, Certification in Organizational Psychology with a focus on Executive Coaching through the Professional School of Psychology in California and MBTI® Personality Type Assessment Qualification from Psychometrics Canada. She is also the author of *The A List: 9 Guiding Principles for Healthy Eating and Positive Living*.

Send Roslyn your comments on how anything
you have read in this book has helped or
enlightened you, or someone you know,
in any way. Please send comments to
roslyn@roslynfranken.com.

To purchase copies of
MEANT TO BE,
and to book Roslyn Franken for
speaking engagements, coaching
and media interviews, visit
www.roslynfranken.com